ACTIVITIES FOR DEVELOPING CONVERSATIONS

STRATEGIES IN SPEAKING

LINGUAL HOUSE

Michael Rost

Published by
Longman Asia ELT
A division of Addison Wesley Longman
2nd Floor, Cornwall House
Taikoo Place
979 King's Road
Quarry Bay
Hong Kong
fax: +852 2856 9578
e-mail: aelt@awl.com.hk

http://www.awl-elt.com

and Associated Companies throughout the world

This book was developed for Longman Asia ELT by Lateral Communications Limited. Lingual House is an imprint of Longman Asia ELT.

First published 1998
Reprinted 1998

Produced by Longman Asia Limited, Hong Kong
NPCC/02

Development editors: Anne McGannon, Lewis Lansford, Linda O'Roke
Project editor: Linda O'Roke
Project coordinator: Keiko Kimura
Project consultant: Melody Noll
Production coordinator: Eric Yau
Text design: Keiko Kimura
Cover design: Keiko Kimura, Lori Margulies
Illustrations: Kari Lehr, Bruce Day, Mark Ziemann
Recording supervisor: David Joslyn
Photograph coordination: Photodisc, Ken Kitamura, Rubberball, Diamar Portfolios

ISBN Textbook 962 00 1422 7
ISBN Teacher's Manual 962 00 1423 5
ISBN Cassette 962 00 1424 3

ABOUT THE AUTHOR

Michael Rost has been active in teaching English, teacher training, and Applied Linguistics research for over 20 years. He has enjoyed teaching in a variety of contexts, including West African high schools, Southeast Asian refugee camps, Japanese intensive language centers, and American teacher training programs. In addition to teaching and teacher training, Michael Rost has been in demand as an educational consultant and as a lecturer. He has worked with the Save the Children Foundation, the Corporation for Public Broadcasting, and DynEd International, and has lectured in numerous countries, including Japan, Korea, Taiwan, Thailand, England, and Denmark. From this range of experiences, he has learned to be sensitive to different students and their purposes for learning languages. Michael Rost is known to teachers internationally as an author of language textbooks (particularly, the *Real Time English* series, *Basics in Listening, Strategies in Listening*), as a development editor (*Impact* Series, *English Firsthand* series), and as an author of Applied Linguistics and teacher training books (*Listening in Language Learning, Listening in Action, Introducing Listening*). Michael has a B.A. in Education (Michigan), M.A. in TESOL (Arizona), and a Ph.D. in Linguistics (Lancaster). He currently lives in San Francisco and teaches at the University of California, Berkeley. You can contact him via e-mail at <mrost@well.com>.

ACKNOWLEDGEMENTS

The author and editors wish to thank the teachers and students who contributed to this project through interviews, reviews, and piloting reports.

In particular, we wish to thank:

Fu-Hsiang Wang	Tim Hawthorne	Stefan Ptak	Karen Sutherland
Cheng-Yuan Liu	Roger Swee	Kevin Trainor	James Ball
Kari Kugler	Damon Chapman	Gareth Magowan	Kate Murphy
Francois Lambert	Cate Crosby	Rachel Wilson	Simon Balint
Ben Dilworth	Steve Coyle	Yu-Shiu Chen	Mei-Yu Chang

Special thanks go to Grant Trew, Akiko Shinagawa, James Boyd, Stephen Ryan, Craig Smith, Won-Key Lee, James Kahny, and Patrick Wallace, who gave ongoing advice on the project.

We would also like to thank the Addison Wesley Longman staff for their support and their valuable advice throughout the development of the project. In particular, we wish to acknowledge Dugie Cameron, Michael Boyd, Barton Armstrong, Jeremy Osborne, Chris Balderston, J.J. Lee, and Betty Teng.

We would like to thank the following individuals and organizations who kindly supplied us with information and permissions to utilize copyrighted material: Psychology Today for permission to quote material from "In Living Color", used on page 18, reprinted with permission from Psychology Today magazine ©1997 (Sussex Publishers, Inc.); The Village Voice for material from their entertainment guide, "Choice", used on page 22; Esquire magazine for material from "My Favorite Thing" used on page 28, first published as "My Favorite Thing" in Esquire magazine, June 1996. Reprinted courtesy of Esquire magazine and the Hearst Corporation; Virtual World Inc., for permission to reprint their brochure on page 32; Roger Daniels for use of information in his book, *Coming to America*, ©1990, Visual Education Corporation, on page 36; Sherwood Schwartz and Gabi Rona for permission to reprint the photograph on page 40; Jon Krakauer and Doubleday Books for use of information in *Into the Wild*, © 1996 Doubleday Books; Psychology Today for permission to adapt material from the article, "Climate Control", reprinted with permission from Psychology Today magazine ©1997 (Sussex Publishers, Inc.); Craig Caldwell and The Blake Street Sports Club, Denver, Colorado, for permission to reprint material from their brochure, on page 54; the American Institute of Stress for information on stress tests; Bryan Mumford, of Santa Barbara, California, for permission to reproduce photographs of his inventions on page 62; International Expeditions Inc. of Helena, Alabama, for permission to reproduce material from their catalogue on page 66; Teen Magazine for material from "Trendflash", used on page 70, ©1996 Teen magazine; Jana Murphy and Pet Life, for permission to use material from "Comedian Jay Leno: One Lucky Guy", first appearing in August 1996, Pet Life ; NBC Entertainment for permission to reprint the photo on page 74; Marc Brown for permission to reproduce drawings from *Hand Rhymes*, ©1985 by Marc Brown.

CONTENTS

INTRODUCTION

Strategies in Speaking: Activities for Developing Conversations is a comprehensive communication course for adult students at intermediate levels. Its companion book, *Basics in Speaking: Activities for Building Conversations,* is intended for students at a beginning level.

The Student Book consists of 18 main units, plus 4 review units ("Fluency Units"), with an appendix containing tape scripts and a vocabulary review. There is a separate audio cassette and a **Teacher's Manual** with suggestions for classroom use and review quizzes.

BALANCED PRACTICE

Each unit provides practice with the **component skills** needed for conversation:
- conversation functions
- selective listening
- pronunciation
- pattern practice
- free conversation
- common phrases
- vocabulary building
- communication tasks

REAL CONTENT

Each unit features **authentic conversational language, real world topics,** and **practical tasks.**

LOW-STRESS INTERACTION

Each activity sets up **easily** for pair work or group work. Activities **satisfy** learners by focusing on both **accuracy** (Conversation, Listening, Pronunciation, Practice) and **fluency** (Exchange, Small Talk, and Communication Task).

RICH VOCABULARY

The course builds up **500 key expressions:**
* formulaic expressions
* functional gambits
* conversational questions

STRUCTURE

The course covers the most **common grammar forms** in spoken English, and integrates them with **everyday functions.**

Each of 18 main units in *Strategies in Speaking* provides a series of 9 short activities to build conversation skills. The sections are designed to be ready to teach without extensive preparation. Following are some basic teaching suggestions. Detailed teaching suggestions are found in the Teacher's Manual.

GRAMMAR TARGETS
- Allow the students a few minutes to review the table on their own. Answer questions about unfamiliar words or grammar structures.
- Ask the **WARM UP** question to begin activating the grammar targets.

1 CONVERSATION
- Ask questions about the picture. Have the students respond individually or as a class.
- Have the students read the conversation and try to complete the blanks. Then listen to the tape to check.
- Have the students practice the conversation with a partner.

2 LISTENING
- Have the students look over the "missing information" before they listen.
- Then ask the students to listen to the tape and complete the information.

3 PRONUNCIATION TIP
- Read over the "how to" advice with the students and review the models.
- Then listen to the tape and have the students practice the pronunciation tip.

4 PRACTICE
- Have the students work with a partner to practice the grammar pattern.
- Review the items with the whole class.

5 EXCHANGE
- Preview the **BASIC CONVERSATION** pattern, the **COMMUNICATION TIP**, and the **BONUS** expressions with the students.
- Then have the students stand up and practice the conversation with several different classmates.

6 VOCABULARY BUILDING
- Have the students work in pairs to complete the vocabulary activity.
- Check the follow-up questions with the whole class.

7 SMALL TALK
- Read the short passage orally with the class.
- Have the students work in small groups to ask and answer the **SMALL TALK** questions.

8 COMMUNICATION TASK
- Have the students work in pairs or small groups to exchange information in order to complete the **COMMUNICATION GOAL**.
- Have the students share the outcome with the whole class.

9 GRAMMAR CHECK
- Have the students work in pairs to complete this grammar check activity.
- Check the answers with the class.

After every 4 or 5 units, there is a review unit called a "Fluency Unit." Here are some suggestions for using the **FLUENCY UNITS**:

TALKING CIRCLES
- Arrange the students in two large circles (or a similar grouping). Each student should face his or her partner and talk about the first topic for one or two minutes.
- Then the students switch partners and talk about the same topic. Repeat this for 3 or 4 partners. Then switch topics.

ROLE PLAY
- Have the students work with a partner. They choose one of the situations and prepare a dialogue.
- After each pair rehearses their dialogue, they act it out in front of the class.

1 Personal Interests

GRAMMAR TARGETS

Finding a Common Topic	What **do** you **do**	for a living?	**I'm an** office worker. **I work for** Chevron.
	What **do** you **do**	in your free time?	I **like to** read. I **enjoy** cook**ing**.
Opinions	How **do** you **like**	your job?	**It's** OK. **It's not** very interesting.
	What **do** you **think** of	this class?	**It's** a little difficult. **It's** interesting.

WARM UP *What do you talk about with your friends?*

1 CONVERSATION

Look at the picture. *Where are they? What is happening?*

Fill in the missing words. Then listen and check your answers.

Gina: _____ in the
_{Are you   Do you}
art department?

Rob: Yeah, _____. Are you?
_{I'm   I am}

Gina: Yeah, _____. How
_{I also am   I am, too}
_____ like it?
_{are you   do you}

Rob: Oh, _____ OK,
_{I'm   it's}
but it's _____ busy.
_{so   such}

Gina: Yeah, I know _____.
_{you mean   what you mean}

Rob: By the way, I'm Rob.

Gina: I'm Gina. Nice to meet you.

Now practice the conversation.

2 LISTENING 📼

Listen and check the correct information.

1. .... They're taking the same class.
   .... They're working for the same company .

   .... They like it.
   .... They don't like it.

2. .... They work in the same office.
   .... They're working on the same project.

   .... They like it.
   .... They don't like it.

3 PRONUNCIATION TIP 📼

YesINo Questions and WH Questions have different melodies. You will sound interested and friendly if you use them correctly.

Yes|No Questions: ⌣
1. Stress the most important word.
   Do you <u>work</u> in the <u>art</u> department?

2. Go up ⌣ at the end of the question.

Do you **work** in the *art department?*

WH Questions: ⌣ ⌢
1. Jump up to the most important word.
   How do you like it?

2. Step down to the end of the question.

Listen. Mark the stressed syllables (■). Mark where your voice goes up (⌣) or up (⌣) and down (⌢).

1. What do you do for a living?
2. Are you in the art department?
3. How do you like it?
4. Do you know Dan?

5. How about you?
6. What are you interested in?
7. What do you do in your free time?
8. What do you think of this class?

Listen again and then repeat.

4 PRACTICE

Work with a partner. Ask and answer the questions.

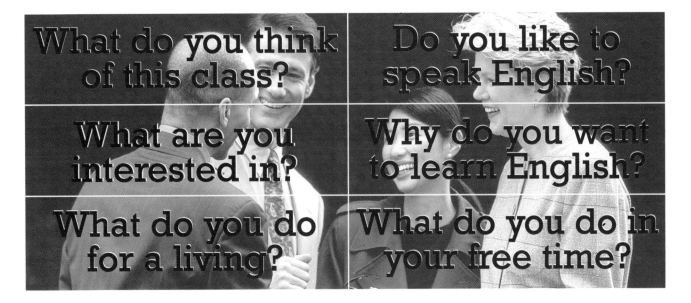

EXAMPLE

What are you interested in?
I like reading.
What do you do in your free time?
I like to visit bookstores.

Write two more questions to ask your partner

• ....

• ....

5 EXCHANGE

Stand up and walk around the class. Introduce yourself to five new classmates.

CULTURE TIP

Make **eye contact** with your partner during the conversation. **Shake hands strongly** when you introduce yourself.

BASIC CONVERSATION

Hi, I'm _____.
Hi, I'm _____.
Nice to meet you.
Nice to meet you, too. What do you think of this class?

BONUS

Try to use some of these expressions.

ASKING
• How do you like this class?
• I like it. How about you?

ANSWERING
• It's great.
• It's not so interesting for me.

FAREWELL (FIRST TIME)
• It was nice meeting you.

6 VOCABULARY BUILDING

Match the questions in Column A and Column B that have a similar meaning.

What are you interested in?
How do you like this class?
What do you do?
Why are you learning English?
What do you do in your free time?
Do you enjoy being a student?
Do you and Tom know each other?
Do you like your job?
Do you and Gina have the same interests?
Where do you come from?

What are you learning English for?
Do you two know each other?
What are your hobbies?
Are both of you interested in the same things?
How is school?
What do you think of this class?
How do you like your job?
What kinds of things are you interested in?
Where are you from?
What do you do for a living?

Now cover the expressions on the right. Can you remember them?

7 SMALL TALK: TOPICS OF CONVERSATION

When people first meet someone at work, at school, or at a social gathering, they usually talk about a few basic topics. Here are some questions that people might ask. Most questions are "safe"; you can ask them to anyone. However, some questions might be considered "dangerous".

Safe questions	Usually safe, but sometimes dangerous	Dangerous questions
• How is your school work going?	• How is your job?	• Do you like your job?
• What do you do (for a living)?	• What do you think about this class?	• Do you make a good salary?
• How do you like living (working) here?	• How is your family?	• Are you married?

Talk about these questions with your classmates.

Why are some topics dangerous?

What are some other "dangerous" topics?

What are some other "safe" topics?

8 COMMUNICATION TASK — *Can I ask you a question?*

Work with a partner. Look at each person. Think of two questions to ask each person: a typical question and an unusual question.

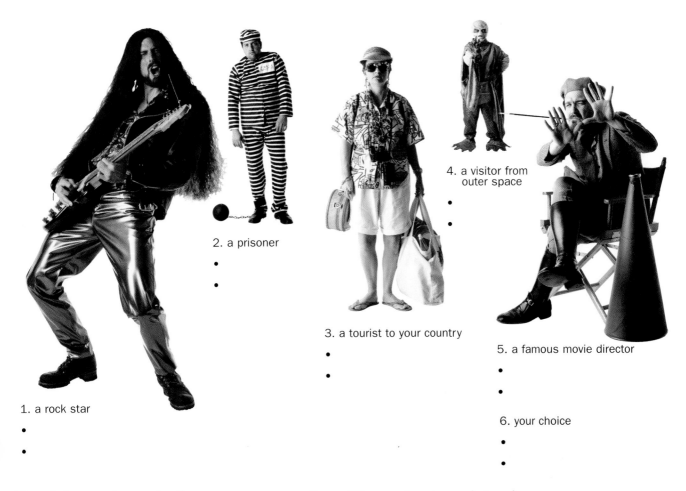

4. a visitor from outer space

2. a prisoner

3. a tourist to your country

5. a famous movie director

1. a rock star

6. your choice

Now join another pair. Compare your questions. Then act out one interview. Which questions were most interesting?

9 GRAMMAR CHECK

Work with a partner. Each conversation has one or two errors. Correct the errors.

1. What are you interested? *in*
   I'm interested in music.^

2. How are you like this class?
   It's OK. It's a little difficult for me.

3. What does Max do?
   He's accountant. He works IBM.

4. What do you think this class?
   I really like it. The teacher is very good.

5. What does Amy do in your free time?
   Her free time she plays sports.

6. What kinds of things are Jon and Mary interested in?
   They're interested many things, especially travel.

7. What does Toru do for a living?
   He's a student Tokyo University.

8. How do you and Tom know each other?
   We're work for the same company.

Now make conversations with the correct sentences.

2 Communication

UNIT

GRAMMAR TARGETS

Asking for Information	Do	you	have	a	fax number? pager?	Yes, it's 555-1212. No, I **don't**.		
	Does	she	have		cell phone?	Yes, she **does**.		
				an	e-mail address?	No, she **doesn't**.		
	What's	your her		number? address?		**It's** 564-8697. **It's** 926 Fulton Road.		
Arranging a Time	When	can	I	call reach	you? her?	**Call**	after 9:30. in the evening.	
	When's the best time **to**			see meet	you? her?	After 9:30 Evenings	**is** **are**	best. best.

WARM UP *What's your phone number? When is the best time to call you?*

1 CONVERSATION 🔊

Look at the picture. *Where are they? What is happening?*

Fill in the missing words. Then listen and check your answers.

Tony: Could I _____ (lend / borrow) your notes from last week's class?

Patty: Sure, but I _____ (haven't / don't have) them with me.

Tony: Oh, no.

Patty: Do you have _____ (a / the) fax machine? I _____ (could / should) fax them to you.

Tony: Yes, I _____ (have / do). That'd _____ (is / be) great.

Patty: What's _____ (you / your) fax number?

Tony: It's 489-0770.

Patty: Got it. I _____ (send / 'll send) them tonight.

Tony: Thanks. You're a real life saver!

Now practice the conversation.

12

2 LISTENING

Listen and write the correct information.

1. Phone number: _____
   Best time to call: _____

2. Office address: _____
   Best time to visit: _____

3 PRONUNCIATION TIP

HOW TO

Stress Compound Nouns

Compound nouns are often difficult to pronounce. Pay attention to stress.

Stress the first word.

■ ▪

Speech Class

Stretch the stressed syllable.

■▪

e-mail

Make the stressed syllable long and clear.

▪ ■ ▪ ▪ ▪

an **answering** machine

Mark the stressed syllable.

1. a fax machine
2. a fax number
3. a phone number
4. a cell phone
5. an e-mail address
6. an office address

Listen again and then repeat.

4 PRACTICE

Work with a partner. Ask your partner the following questions.

EXAMPLE

What's your phone number?
It's 489-0770.
When's the best time to call you?
Between 8 and 10.

5 EXCHANGE

Walk around the class. Talk to your classmates.
Ask each person for a favor.

CULTURE TIP

Express your appreciation. **"That's great. Thanks a lot."**

BASIC CONVERSATION

Hi, _____. Can I ask you a favor?
Sure. What is it?
I don't have _____.
I can send them to you.
That's great. I'll give you my _____.
It's _____.

BONUS

Try to use some of these expressions.

ASKING A FAVOR
• Excuse me, can I ask you a favor?
• Hi. I wonder if I can ask you something.

ENDING THE CONVERSATION
• Nice talking to you. See you later.
• Thanks a lot. I appreciate it.

IF YOU DON'T UNDERSTAND
• Sorry, could you say that again?
• Excuse me. I didn't catch that.

6 VOCABULARY BUILDING

Match the expression on the left with a similar expression on the right.

When's the best time to call you?	When do you want to meet?
I don't have a fax number.	Sorry, I didn't catch that.
That's great.	I appreciate it.
Is it OK to call you at home?	Will you do something for me?
When can I see you?	I missed yesterday's class.
Do you have a pager?	Can I call you at home?
Could you please say that again?	What time should I call you?
Can I ask you a favor?	Wonderful!
I wasn't in class yesterday.	I don't own a fax machine.
Thanks a lot.	Can I get your pager number?

7 SMALL TALK: MODERN COMMUNICATION

Early forms of long-distance communication used sight and sound: drums in Africa, horns in Switzerland, and smoke signals by Native Americans. Now most people use electronic forms of communication.

TYPE OF COMMUNICATION	Do you like to use it?	Yes	No	I never use it
	a telephone			
	a cellular phone			
	a car phone			
	a video phone			
	e-mail			
	a pager (beeper)			
	an Internet web site			
	an on-line "chat room"			
	audio messages (answer machines)			
	video messages			
	letters			

Talk about these questions with your classmates.

What are some other ways to contact people?

Do you think fast communication is good?

What do you think one future form of communication will be?

8 COMMUNICATION TASK  Your "Home Page"

You are going to design a Home Page. A Home Page is a way to introduce yourself.
Think about each item for your Home Page.

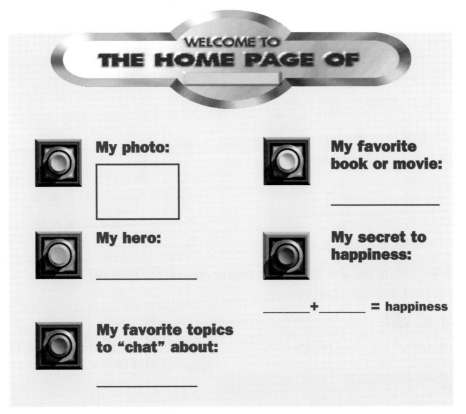

Work in a group of four. Show your Home Page to your partners.
Ask questions about your partners' information.
Show your Home Pages to the class.

9 GRAMMAR CHECK

Make questions to match each answer.

1. .... fax number?
   Yes, it's 549-7841.

2. .... address?
   It's 511 Marshall Street.

3 .... you?
   Please call between 9 and 10 p.m.

4. .... call you at home?
   Sure, it's OK. Call me anytime.

5. .... fax machine?
   Yes, I have one, but I hardly ever use it.

6. Do you have .... ?
   Yes, it's tomcat@aol.com.

7. .... 781-2002?
   No, it's 781-2020.

8. .... fax machine?
   No, sorry. I don't have one.

9. .... tell me your
   phone number?
   Yes, it's 211-655-9128.

10. .... in your office?
    Sure. Please stop by in the afternoon.

Now practice the conversations.

3 Impressions

GRAMMAR TARGETS

Compliments	That's	**a** nice	jacket.	Thanks.			
	Those are	beautiful	earrings.	Oh, thank you.			
	I really	**like** **love**	your that those	jacket. dress shoes.			
Asking about something	Where **did** you	**get** **buy**	that jacket? it?	I	**got**	it	**for** my birthday. **at** Macy's. **from** my friend.
	Is that jacket new?			Yes,	my brother sister friend	**gave** **lent** **bought**	it to me. it for me.

WARM UP *How do you get "first impressions" of people? Think of 5 ideas.*
Example: clothes

1 CONVERSATION

Look at the picture. *Where are they? What is happening?*

Fill in the missing words. Then listen and check your answers.

Judy: Rich, is _____ you?
                    that   there

Rich: Oh, hi, Judy.

Judy: I didn't _____ you.
                 remember   recognize

Rich: Oh, it _____ be my
               must   will
new hairstyle.

Judy: Yeah, _____ it.
            that's   is

Rich: Well, how _____
                are   do
you like it?

Judy: Oh, it's...um...very

_____.
interested   interesting

Rich: Thanks. I'm glad you like it.

Now practice the conversation.

2 LISTENING 📼

Listen and write the correct information. What item do they talk about?
What do they say about it?

1. Item: ....
   What they say: ....

2. Item: ....
   What they say: ....

3 PRONUNCIATION TIP 📼

you	your
When "you" is unstressed, say /yə/.	When "your" is unstressed, say /yər/.

HOW TO
Reduce "you" and "your"

Reductions are an important part of clear pronunciation. Making pronouns short will improve your English rhythm. Use the schwa sound /ə/ to help you. This short little vowel sounds like the noise you make when you pick up something heavy.

Listen. Mark the stressed syllables.

1. like it
   yə like it
   How do yə like it?

2. talking about
   yə talking about
   What are yə talking about?

3. notice
   yə notice
   Didn't yə notice?

4. don't like it
   yə don't like it
   But yə don't like it?

5. hair style
   yər new hair style
   Oh, yər new hair style!

6. beautiful
   earrings are beautiful
   Yər earrings are beautiful!

7. ring
   yər ring
   I like yər ring.

8. like it
   glad yə like it
   I'm glad yə like it.

Listen again and repeat.

4 PRACTICE

Work with a partner. Give your partner a compliment on 5 things.
Don't use the same compliment twice!
Don't use the same response twice.

COMPLIMENTS	RESPONSES
You have a nice...	Thank you./Thanks.
I really like your...	Oh, thanks.
What a nice...!	Thanks for noticing.
I love your...	I'm glad you like it.

5 EXCHANGE

Stand up and walk around the class.
Give one compliment to each person.

BASIC CONVERSATION

Hi, I really like your ring.
> *Thanks. I got it for my 20th birthday.*
Well, it's really beautiful.

CULTURE TIP

It's OK to accept a compliment.
"That's a nice tie."
"Oh, thanks. I'm glad you like it."

BONUS

Try to use some of these expressions.

COMPLIMENTS
• Your earrings are beautiful.
• Hey, that's a great jacket.

RESPONSES
• Oh, thanks for noticing.
• I'm glad you like it.

STATEMENTS
• It's nothing special.
• It's my favorite shirt.
• It was a gift.

6 VOCABULARY BUILDING

Put these words and phrases in the correct column.

It's...

awful	great	not my type	super	dreadful
pretty strange	kind of nice	OK	terrible	unusual
fantastic	lousy	OK, I guess	terrific	lovely
good				

very negative	somewhat negative	somewhat positive	very positive

Can you add one more word or phrase to each column?

7 SMALL TALK: COLORS AND EMOTIONS

Norma Kamali is a fashion designer who emphasizes color. According to Ms. Kamali, "Color is inspirational. Dressing with color is a much different experience than dressing in black. Color is like the sun—it's full of light and reflection. It's optimistic and fertile." Here are some of the most popular colors, and how many people say these colors make them feel:

healthy, vibrant   **energetic, fresh**   **friendly, nice**   **young, spontaneous**

relaxed, comfortable   **powerful, strong**   **isolated, individualistic**   **passionate, romantic**

Talk about these questions with your classmates.

What are your favorite colors?

Do colors influence your mood?

Do you prefer any special types of clothes? Why?

18

8 COMMUNICATION TASK  First impressions

Write one or two words — your first impressions — about each person.

Now work in a group of 4. Compare your "first impressions."
Ask your partners to explain their answers.
With your partners, decide: Which person would you like to meet?
Make up some information about him or her.

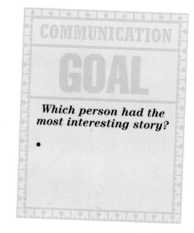

COMMUNICATION

GOAL

*Which person had the
most interesting story?*

•

name	• ....
nationality	• ....
job	• ....
how you met him or her	• ....
something special about him or her	• ....

Now present your information to the class.

9 GRAMMAR CHECK

Match each question with the best answer.

Who gave those to you?   I bought it at Macy's.
Where did you get that ring?   Actually, I don't remember who.
Do you like the new dress I got you?   I don't remember exactly, but it wasn't very expensive.
How do you like my new sweater?   Yes, my wife gave it to me for my birthday.
How much did that cost?   I don't really like them.
What do you think of these shoes?   I like the green one.
Was that sweater a present?   No, I got it at Isetan.
Is that a new necklace?   Oh, I love it. Thanks again.
Which belt do you like best?   It's very nice!
Did you get that ring at Macy's?   No, I've had this for a long time.

Now practice the conversations.

4 Weekends

GRAMMAR TARGETS

Wh- questions	What	**did**	you Jack Mike and Lisa		**do**	on Saturday? last weekend?	We He	**went** **visited**	to a movie. his relatives.
	Where	**did**	you he they	**go**		on Sunday?	I He They	**went** **stayed**	to my friend's house. at home.
	When	**did**	they	**go**		to the movie?	They	**went**	(on) Sunday. last night.
Yes-No Questions	**Did**	you he they	**go** **have** **play**	to the movies? a date? tennis?			Yes, No,	I he they	**did.** **didn't.**

WARM UP *What did you do last weekend? What do you usually do on the weekend?*

1 CONVERSATION 🎙️

Look at the picture. *Where are they? What is happening?*

Fill in the missing words. Then listen and check your answers.

Carine: Hi, Jon. How _____ your weekend?
_{is   was}

Jon: It was pretty dull. I didn't do _____. How about you?
_{many   much}

Carine: Well, I _____ to the
_{did   went}
company party on Saturday night.

Jon: Oh, the company party. Darn! I forgot all about _____!
_{that   those}
How was it?

Carine: It was fun. There was a _____ of good food and
_{lot   lots}
good music.

Jon: _____ sorry I missed it.
_{I was   I'm}

Now practice the conversation.

2 LISTENING

Listen and write the correct information. Where did they go? How was it?

1. Jessica went to _____.   2. Jason went to _____.

   It was _____.   It was _____.

3 PRONUNCIATION TIP

HOW TO

Say an American /t/

When /t/ comes between two vowel sounds, you can pronounce it as a quick /d/ sound. This will help you to speak American English more naturally.

Change /t/ to /d/ in the middle of a word when /t/ immediately follows the stressed syllable:

d
↑
party

You can also change /t/ to /d/ in a word connection:

d
↑
There was a **lot** of good **food**.

Underline the /d/ sounds.

1. pretty   5. better
2. Saturday   6. later
3. water   7. computer
4. city   8. British

Now listen again and repeat.

Listen and repeat:

1. go *da*
   go *da* the
   go *da* the **mo**vies
   Did you go to
   the **mo**vies?

2. d all
   d all a**bout** that!
   forgot all a**bout**
     that!
   I forgot all a**bout**
     that!

4 PRACTICE

Work with a partner. Ask about his or her activities last weekend.

EXAMPLE

What did you do last Friday night?
    I went to a movie with a friend.
How was it?
    It was fun.

Friday night

Saturday night

Saturday morning

Sunday during the day

Saturday afternoon

Sunday night

5 EXCHANGE

Stand up and walk around the class.
Ask your classmates about their activities last weekend.

BASIC CONVERSATION

How was your weekend?
It was OK.
What did you do on Friday night?
I went to a party with a friend.

BONUS

Try to use some of these expressions.

RESPONDING
• Saturday was pretty good, but Sunday wasn't so interesting.

RESPONDING TO INFORMATION
• Sounds like fun.
• I wish I had gone with you.

REVERSING THE QUESTION
• How about you?
• Tell me what you did.

6 VOCABULARY BUILDING

Put these time expressions in order.

- a minute ago
- over 100 years ago
- yesterday
- an hour ago
- a few days ago
- at 2 a.m. today
- on my last birthday
- before I was born
- last week
- a month ago
- in 1995
- 70 years ago
- the year I was born
- last weekend
- the day before yesterday

long ago   *over 100 years ago*

....
....
....
....
....
....
....
                    a minute ago
now

7 SMALL TALK: WEEKEND ACTIVITIES

Many people claim they have nothing to do on the weekend. Here is a recent list of activities from a Summer Weekend Guide.

WEEKEND

- antique market
- aquarium tour
- ballet
- baseball game
- cartoon art museum
- comedy club
- dance club
- dog show
- farmer's market
- fashion exposition

- meet the authors event at a bookstore
- movies
- museum
- nightclub
- photography exhibit
- rock concert
- rose gardening demonstration
- symphony
- salsa dance lessons

- gallery opening
- historical society exhibition
- introductory ceramics class
- lecture on health
- magic show
- walking tour of the city
- zoo
- martial arts exhibition
- cultural festival
- theater

GUIDE

Talk about these questions with your classmates.

Which of these activities are interesting to you?

Which of these activites would you do if they were free?

8 COMMUNICATION TASK — Weekend Activities Game

Play this game in a group of three or four. Take turns.

STEPS

❶ Move around the board to the next open square.
❷ When you stop on a square, ask 3 different questions about the topic to your partners.
❸ If you can ask a question to each one, you get three points.
❹ If you can answer each question, you get one point.

Sample questions for: *an indoor activity*
Do you like (bowling)?
How often do you (go bowling)?
Would you like to (go bowling) tonight?
What do you think of (bowling)?
Do you ever (go bowling)?
Where can you (go bowling)?

START →

| 1 an indoor activity | 2 an activity for a rainy day | 3 an activity to do in the snow | 4 an activity in a car | 5 a night-time activity | 6 an outdoor activity | 7 a summer-time activity |

Weekend Activities GAME

18 a holiday activity — 8 an activity to do with a lot of people
17 an activity you do alone — 9 a romantic activity
16 a free activity — 15 an activity that costs a lot of money — 14 an activity you do with your family — 13 an activity you do in the park — 12 a sports activity — 11 an exciting activity — 10 a boring activity

9 GRAMMAR CHECK

Using the clues given, make correct questions in the past tense.

1. ....
   go - where - last weekend

2. ....
   who - go with - concert

3. ....
   which - restaurant - eat - last Saturday

4. ....
   where - go - date - Cindy - and

5. ....
   see - movie - Volcano

6. ....
   roller-skating - park - your friends - Sunday

7. ....
   have a party - your house - last weekend

8. ....
   weekend - relaxing

9. ....
   have dinner - family - last night - with

Now ask the questions to your partner. Your partner will answer.

ACTIVITY 1 SPEAKING CIRCLES

GRAMMAR TARGETS

WH QUESTIONS		
What	**What** are you interested in?	I'm interested in **music**.
Who	**Who** is your favorite singer?	**Tracy Chapman** is.
Why	**Why** do you like her?	**Because** she **has** a beautiful voice.
Where	**Where** did you go on Friday?	I **went to Southland Music Club**.
When	**When** did you get home?	I got home **at 11:30**.
Which	**Which** CD did you buy?	I bought **Wild Roses**.

❶ Sit in two rows. Face each other.
❷ Start with TOPIC 1.
❸ Talk to your partner for 1 minute.
❹ Then change partners.
❺ Talk for 1 minute about the same topic.
❻ Continue for 3 or 4 partners.
❼ Start again on TOPIC 2 with a new partner.

TOPIC 1

INTERESTS

Sample questions:
What is one special thing item you own?
Have you seen a lap top computer before?
Do you own a lot of things?

TOPIC 2

COMMUNICATION

Sample questions:
Do you have a fax machine?
When's the worst time to call you?
Which do you like most: talking on the phone, writing letters, or using e-mail?
How often do you talk to people in English?

TOPIC 3

WEEKENDS

Sample questions:
Where did you go last weekend?
What did you do Friday night?
Did you see a movie?
What is the best weekend activity for you?

CONVERSATION
TIP
Don't worry about making mistakes. Keep talking.

TOPIC 4

IMPRESSIONS

Sample questions:
Where did you get that (watch)?
What was your first impression of our teacher?
What do you notice first when you meet a new person?
Why do people care so much about their clothes?

ACTIVITY 2 ROLE PLAY

Work with a partner. Choose a situation. Make up a dialogue.
Practice your dialogue. Then say your dialogue in front of the class.

CULTURE TIP

Don't be afraid to use your English. Try some new expressions.

EXAMPLE

Two classmates talking about their class.

Karen: What do you think of this class?
Steph: *I like it. How about you?*
Karen: I like it, too, but the speaking exercises are a little difficult.
Steph: *Yeah, I know what you mean.*

SITUATION 1

Two people meet at Paul's party.

Possible Expressions:

Hi, my name's. . .

We both work for. . .

How do you know Paul?

Are you interested in. . .?

SITUATION 2

One friend suggests a travel agent to another friend.

Possible Expressions:

What's the agency's phone number?

Do they have a fax number?

The best time to call is. . .

I always buy tickets there.

SITUATION 3

Two friends meet for dinner. One friend has on a new outfit. The other has a new haircut.

Possible Expressions:

That looks great on you.

Where did you get that outfit?

Thanks, I got it . . .

Do you like it?

SITUATION 4

Two co-workers talk about their weekends.

Possible Expressions:

Did you have a nice weekend?

What did you do on. . .?

It was fun but went by too quickly.

Friday night I went to. . .

5 Personal Items

GRAMMAR TARGETS

Asking	What	**does** **do**	it they	**look** like?	What What How	color **is** it? **is** it made of? big **is** it?
	It**'s** They**'re**	square. round			It**'s** They**'re**	**made** of	leather. plastic.
Describing	My purse It	**is**	black. brown.		My wallet It	**has**	stripes. my name on it.
	His shoes They	**are**	blue pink.		His pants They	**have**	a flower pattern. big pockets.
Comparisons	My pen It	is	new**er** **more** expensive	**than**	your pen. yours.
	Your shoes They	are	**more** comfortable **less** expensive	**than**	my shoes. mine.

WARM UP *Choose one object in the classroom. Think of five words or expressions to describe it.*

1 CONVERSATION

Look at the picture. *Where are they? What is happening?*

Fill in the missing words. Then listen and check your answers.

Lisa: What's _____ in your hand?
_{it   that}

Bill: It's _____ . I got
_{a clock   a watch}
it _____ my grandfather.
_{of   from}

Lisa: Oh, it _____ very old.
_{sees   looks}
Can I _____ it?
_{watch   see}

Bill: _____ .
_{Sure   Surely}

Lisa: Oh, it's _____ . It's
_{beautiful   beauty}
so _____ and _____ .
_{smooth   smoothness   shine   shiny}

Bill: I think it's _____
_{made   making}
of gold. I really like it.

Now practice the conversation.

26

2 LISTENING 📟

Listen and write the correct information. What item are they talking about? What does it look like?

1. Item: ....
   Description:
   - ....
   - ....

2. Item: ....
   Description:
   - ....
   - ....

3 PRONUNCIATION TIP 📟

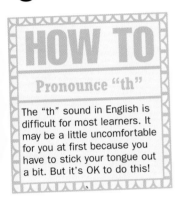

HOW TO Pronounce "th"

The "th" sound in English is difficult for most learners. It may be a little uncomfortable for you at first because you have to stick your tongue out a bit. But it's OK to do this!

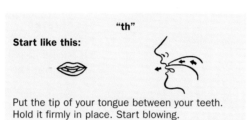

"th"

Start like this:

Put the tip of your tongue between your teeth. Hold it firmly in place. Start blowing.

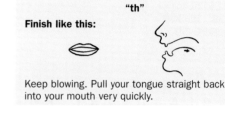

"th"

Finish like this:

Keep blowing. Pull your tongue straight back into your mouth very quickly.

There are two types of "th": /θ/ and /∂/.

To say /θ/ as in "thing", blow out a lot of air. Don't use your voice.

To say /∂/ as in "that", blow out less air. Turn on your voice. Hum as you say it.

Listen to the "th" sounds in the sentences below. Do you hear /θ/ or /∂/? Check (✔) the sound you hear.

/θ/ /∂/
1. ❑ ❑ What's **th**at?
2. ❑ ❑ What's that **th**ing in your hand?
3. ❑ ❑ I got it from my grandfa**th**er.
4. ❑ ❑ It's so smoo**th** and shiny.

/θ/ /∂/
5. ❑ ❑ I **th**ink it's made of gold.
6. ❑ ❑ It has a **th**ick leather band.
7. ❑ ❑ The carrying case has **th**ree big pockets.
8. ❑ ❑ **Th**ey're striped.

Listen again and repeat.

4 PRACTICE

Work with a partner. Tell your partner about six things that you own. Describe each one. Use two words or phrases.

EXAMPLE

Do you have something that is old?
        Yes, I have a _____.
What does it look like?
        It's _____.

something
old
•
•

something
expensive
•
•

something you use
every day
•
•

something
small
•
•

something
electronic
•
•

something
collectible
•
•

5 EXCHANGE

Stand up. Walk around the class.
Ask your classmates about the things they own.

BASIC CONVERSATION

Tell me about something you own.
  OK. I'll tell you about my _____.
What does it look like?
  It's...

BONUS

Try to use some of these expressions.

OPENING
- Can you tell me about something you have?

GETTING INFORMATION
- What does it look like?
- Can you describe it for me?

DESCRIBING
- It's kind of like a...
- It looks like a...
- It's about the size of a...

6 VOCABULARY BUILDING

Put these words and phrases into the correct row.

It's...

tiny	not so big	really big	gigantic	the biggest one
really tiny	huge	pretty big	little	I've ever seen
rather small	enormous	incredibly large	super small	

small					
large					

Can you add one more word or phrase to each row?

7 SMALL TALK: SPECIAL THINGS

I have never owned anything better than a dog, a bicycle, or a radio. My favorite radio was one of the original Sony single-speaker models with an earplug. I remember listening to KPPC, the world's first "underground" radio station. In 1972, I moved out of my parents' house. I left the radio behind and never saw it again.

David Lee Roth,
musician

Talk about these questions with your classmates.

What is something special that you own?

Why is it special?

8 COMMUNICATION TASK  *What is it?*

Work in a group of 4. Think of one special item that you have.
Try to guess the other people's special item.
Ask only *yes-no* questions. Count the questions it takes to guess the item.

> ### EXAMPLE
>
> **Questions**
> Is it large or small?   Is it in your home?
> Do you use it often?   Is it bigger than my hand?

number of guesses   name

what was the item

number of guesses   name

what was the item

number of guesses   name

what was the item

number of guesses   name

what was the item

9 GRAMMAR CHECK

Work with a partner. Choose two items. Make a comparison statement.
Your partner will write your sentence.
Example: Your ring is smaller than your watch.

1. ....
2. ....
3. ....
4. ....
5. ....
6. ....
7. ....
8. ....

GRAMMAR TARGETS

Making Plans	Would you **like to**	**go to** a movie? **see** a play? **go** dancing?		Sorry, I **have to**	study. cook dinner. work.
	Do you **want to**	**meet** for coffee **see** a play **go** bowling	tonight? tomorrow? next weekend?	Yes, sure. That sounds good. OK.	
Deciding on a Place	Where's	**a** fun cheap	music club? restaurant?	Harvey's The Spaghetti Factory	**is** fun. cheap.
	What's	**a** popular good	bar? theater?	T.J.'s The Plaza Theater	**is** popular. good.
Deciding on a Time	When	**should** we leave? **do you want to** leave?		We **should** **leave** **Let's**	around 10:00. at 8:45.

WARM UP *Can you think of five types of entertainment?*
Example: going to a movie

1 CONVERSATION 📼

Now look at the picture. *Where are they? What is happening?*

Fill in the missing words. Then listen and check your answers.

Amber: What do you want
.... tonight?
   to do   doing

Jason: I don't know. Maybe see
.... movie?
  a   the

Amber: Yeah, ... good idea.
      that's   that's a
.... see *Mystery Date*.
Let's   We're going to

Jason: *Mystery Date*? No, I don't
want to .... that.
        see   look

Amber: Come on. .... fun.
            It's   It'll be

Jason: Oh, OK.

Amber: There's a .... at 9:15.
         show   play

Jason: All right. ....
         Let's go   We'll go

Now practice the conversation.

2 LISTENING 📟

Listen and write the correct information. What do they decide to do?

1. Troy and Lisa: ....

2. Lori and Ron: ....

3 PRONUNCIATION TIP 📟

HOW TO

Reduce
"want to" + verb

In conversation, make "want to" and "wants to" weak. This will help your speech sound smooth and natural.

"want to" + verb

1. Stress the most important word.

2. Say "wanna" /wanə/ for "want to".

3. Say "wansta" /wanstə/ for "wants to". Keep these phrases weak.

What do you want to **do** tonight?

I *wanna* see a **movie**.

He *wansta* see a **movie**.

Listen. You will hear some sentences with careful pronunciation, then relaxed pronunciation. Repeat them with relaxed pronunciation. Use "wanna" and "wansta."

*Use "wanna" and "wansta" when you speak. Use "want to" and "wants to" when you write.

4 PRACTICE

Work with a partner.
Think of six entertainment activities in your city or area. Invite your partner to each activity.

EXAMPLE

Would you like to _____?
    OK. When should we go?
Let's go on Saturday.
    Good idea.

Now ask your partner:

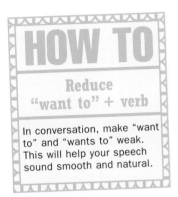

go for a drive to

go to see

have a meal at

go on a date to

take a walk around

have a drink at

5 EXCHANGE

Walk around the class. Invite your classmates to an activity. To make this a game, *don't accept any invitations.* Give an excuse for each invitation.

CULTURE TIP

Keep talking. Give a reason. **"I can't go tonight. I have to..."**

BASIC CONVERSATION

Hi, ____. Would you like to ___ with me?
Oh, I'm sorry, I can't. I have to ....
OK. Maybe some other time.
Sure. See you later.

BONUS

Try to use some of these expressions.

INVITING
• If you're not busy, would you like to...
• I wonder if you'd like to...

RESPONDING: NO
• Sorry, I can't. Can I have a raincheck*?
• Thanks for asking, but I can't.
(* Can we go another time?)

EXCUSES
• I'm meeting my parents for dinner.
• I'll be out of town that day.
• I have other plans that day.

6 VOCABULARY BUILDING

Complete each excuse.

Sorry, I can't go with you because...

I have to give my dog ...	some things at the grocery store
I have to take my mother...	my room
I have to pick up ...	a bath
I have to study ...	my grandmother
I have to do ...	dinner for my family
I have to clean up....	for a test
I have to take care of...	some phone calls
I have to return...	to bed early
I have to make...	to dinner
I have to go...	my laundry

Make up two more excuses.

• ....

• ....

7 SMALL TALK: ENTERTAINMENT FADS

Virtual World™ is one of many electronic entertainment centers that became popular in the 1990s. When you enter, you select a "simulation" room for a 30-minute computerized adventure. The most popular simulations are "Battletech" (a 31st-century war game) and "Red Planet" (a piloting test deep inside an alien planet). Soon to come are other simulations involving time travel and communication with UFOs.

Why is this kind of entertainment so popular? Rich Lewis, a frequent visitor, says, "It's a great form of escape. You can go somewhere you've never been before and be someone else for a while." Another frequent flyer, Cindy Vega, says, "It's much more challenging than sports and much more interesting than dating guys."

Talk about these questions with your classmates.

> What is a new form
> of entertainment
> in your city?

> Do you like it?
> Why or why not?

8 COMMUNICATION TASK   *Entertainment options*

Work with a partner. Read the questions.
Can you think of at least two places for each question?

What's a "hot night spot" in this city?
-
-
-

What's a fun sporting event to see?
-
-
-

What's a good park to go to?
-
-
-

COMMUNICATION GOAL

What new place will you try?
-

What's a nice inexpensive restaurant to eat at?
-
-
-

What is a cool place to go dancing?
-
-
-

What's an elegant place to have dinner?
-
-
-

Where is a popular place to hang out with friends if you don't have any money?
-
-
-

Write two more questions. Then ask your partner to answer them:

- What's a _____ place to _____ ?
- What's a _____ place to _____ ?

Write your favorite places on the board.

9 GRAMMAR CHECK

Put the lines in order to make a conversation.

_____ A: Then are you free on Saturday night?
_____ A: Oh, how about Saturday afternoon?
_____ B: Oh, no. I can't. This Sunday I have to visit my grandmother.
_11_ A: Well, maybe some other time.
_____ B: Oh, sorry. I can't. I'm supposed to go shopping with some friends.
_____ B: Oh, sorry. On Friday night, I have to work. I have a part-time job.
_____ B: Oh, sorry. That's a special night for me. I always have dinner at my brother's house.
_____ A: Then let's go on Sunday.
_____ B: This weekend?
_1_ A: Would you like to go to a movie with me this weekend?
_____ A: Yes, we could go on Friday night.

Now practice the conversation with a partner.

7 Nationality

GRAMMAR TARGETS

Countries	Where	**were you** **was she**	born?				**I was** born in China. **She was** born in the U.S.
	What country	**do you** come from? **does he** come from?					**I come** from Japan. **He comes** from Mexico.
Regions and Cities	What	part of the country state city	**do** you **do** they **does** he	**come** from?	I **come** They **come** He **comes**	from	France. Texas. Tokyo.
Missing	**Do** you (ever)	**get** homesick? **miss** your hometown?		I	sometimes often	**get** homesick. **miss** my hometown. **do**.	
	Does she	**get** homesick? **miss** her hometown?		She She	never always	**gets** homesick. **misses** home. **does**.	

W A R M   U P   *Do you miss anything about your hometown? What?*

1 CONVERSATION 📼

Look at the picture. *Where are they? What is happening?*

Fill in the missing words. Then listen and check your answers.

Kate: May, you're from Thailand, _____ you?

don't   aren't

May: No, I'm from _____ .

China   Chinese

Kate: Oh, you're _____ .

China   Chinese

I _____ know that.

don't   didn't

May: Yeah, I was _____

born   birth

in a small city near Shanghai.

Kate: _____ China?

Do you miss   Are you missing

May: Of course, but I go back from time to time.

Now practice the conversation.

34

2 LISTENING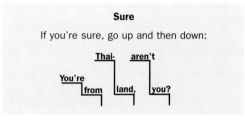

Listen and write the correct information. Where are they from? What do they miss?

1. Pavel
   From: ....
   Misses: ....

2. Maria
   From: ....
   Misses: ....

3 PRONUNCIATION TIP

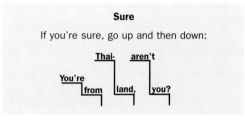

Sure
If you're sure, go up and then down:

Not Sure
If you're not sure, go up at the end:

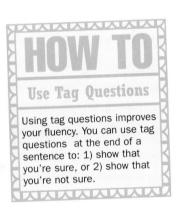

HOW TO

Use Tag Questions

Using tag questions improves your fluency. You can use tag questions at the end of a sentence to: 1) show that you're sure, or 2) show that you're not sure.

Listen. How sure is the speaker? Check (✔) the correct box.

Sure	Not sure	
❏	❏	1. China is a beautiful country, isn't it?
❏	❏	2. You were born near Shanghai, weren't you?
❏	❏	3. You speak Chinese, don't you?
❏	❏	4. Your grandparents aren't in the States, are they?
❏	❏	5. It isn't tough being away from home, is it?
❏	❏	6. It costs a lot to go back and forth, doesn't it?

Listen again and repeat.

4 PRACTICE

Work with a partner. Ask about his or her hometown.

EXAMPLE

Where do you come from?
   I'm from _____.

Where do you come from?

How long did you live there?

Where is it?

Did you like living there?

What do you miss about it?

Do you go back there sometimes?

5 EXCHANGE

**Stand up. Walk around the class. Talk to your classmates.
Ask them about their hometown or where they come from.**

BONUS

Try to use some of these expressions.

ASKING
- What's the biggest difference between your hometown and here?

ANSWERING
- The biggest difference is...

RESPONDING TO SAD INFORMATION
- Oh, I'm sorry to hear that.

GETTING MORE INFORMATION
- Why?
- Oh, really? What's that like?
- I'm not familiar with that.

CULTURE TIP

Cooperate with your partner. Be sure your partner understands you. **"Did I answer your question?"**

BASIC CONVERSATION

Hi, can I ask you a few questions?
Sure. About what?
About your hometown. What is your hometown?
It's _____.

6 VOCABULARY BUILDING

Can you give three associations for each country?

EXAMPLES

name of a place in the country
name of a tourist attraction in that country
name of a famous person from that country
name of something famous from that country

U.S.A. ....
England ....
China ....
France ....
another country: ....

another country: ....

Now read your list of associations to the class. Can they guess the country quickly?

7 SMALL TALK: NATIONAL PERSONALITIES

According to historian Roger Daniels, each country has some key concepts that make up its "personality." According to Daniels, one key concept for the U.S. is "choice."

Most people who came to America in the 1800s and the 1900s came by choice: they chose to come to America. They wanted to build a new life: to choose where to live, what to do, what to think. In a sense, they wanted to choose a new identity. This idea of "choice" is still important to most Americans. It is part of the personality of the country.

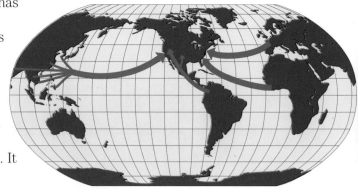

Talk about these questions with your classmates.

Can you think of another key word to describe the U.S.?

What key word describes your country?

8 COMMUNICATION TASK — *National Personalities*

Work in a group of four.
Think of some famous people in your country. They can be living or dead.

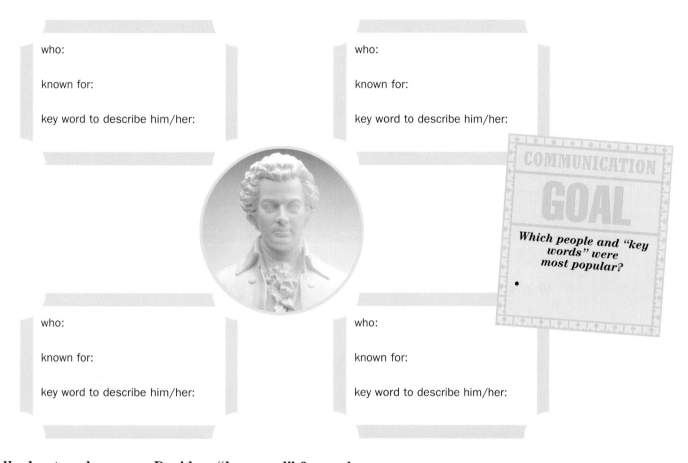

who:

known for:

key word to describe him/her:

who:

known for:

key word to describe him/her:

who:

known for:

key word to describe him/her:

who:

known for:

key word to describe him/her:

COMMUNICATION GOAL
Which people and "key words" were most popular?

Talk about each person. Decide a "key word" for each person.
Next, pair up with someone from another group. Explain your choices.

9 GRAMMAR CHECK

Fill in the blanks with a verb. Use the correct tense.

Hello. My name _____ Ramon. I _____ born in Mexico in 1984.
              is   was   is   was

My family _____ in Mexico until I _____ 14 years old. When I _____ 14,
            live   lived   am   was   am   was

my parents _____ to _____ to the States. Life in the States _____ very
            was decide decided move moved   is   was

different from Mexico. In Mexico we _____ with my grandmother, my grandfather, and many
                                     have lived used to live

of my cousins. Here in the States I only _____ with my mother and father. I _____ my
                                          am living live   miss am missing

family a lot. Sometimes I _____ homesick and _____ to _____ to Mexico, but
                          get am getting   want wanted return returning

sometimes I _____ it here so much that I _____ imagine leaving.
             love am loving   can't couldn't

8 Home

UNIT

GRAMMAR TARGETS

General Description	What's	your her their	new	apartment place house	like?		It's	beautiful. small. unusual.
Specific Description	Do	you they	**have**	a	nice kitchen? big yard?		Yes, Yes,	it **has**	a large window. a lot of trees.
	Does	he she		a	small living room? pretty apartment?		No, No,	it **is**	pretty big. really messy.
Giving Locations	There's	**a**	sofa bed table	**next to across from near**	the window. the door. the TV.			
	There **are**		chairs books	**beside on**	the wall. the bookcase.			

W A R M   U P   *What is your favorite room in your house? Can you describe it?*

1 CONVERSATION 🔲

Look at the picture. *Where are they? What is happening?*

Fill in the missing words. Then listen and check your answers.

Noah: Do you like _____
      _a   _{your}
new apartment?

Andy: Yeah, it's OK. It's much
better _____ my old place.
    _{than}   _{from}

Noah: _____ it like?
   _{What's}   _{What does}

Andy: It's _____ big, and
      _{lovely}   _{pretty}
_____ a great view of the park.
_{it's got}   _{it's with}

Noah: Is it _____ the
         _{close}   _{close to}
train station?

Andy: Yeah, it's _____ close.
         _{very}   _{such}
It's _____ a minute away.
   _{just}   _{yet}

Noah: Sounds perfect.

Now practice the conversation.

2 LISTENING 📟

Listen and write the correct information. What do they say about their home?

1. Tony's apartment

2. Hilary's house

3 PRONUNCIATION TIP 📟

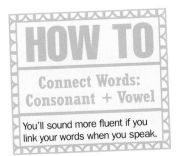

HOW TO

Connect Words:
Consonant + Vowel

You'll sound more fluent if you link your words when you speak.

If a word ends in a consonant sound and the next word begins
with a vowel sound, make a word connection.

d
↑
It's jus**t** a minu**te** away.   *It's justa minuda way.*

Listen and repeat. Speak smoothly. Keep your voice going.

1. zit
   Is it
   Is it close
   Is it close to the **train** station?

2. just a
   just a minute
   just a minute a
   just a minute **away**
   It's just a minute **away**.

3. s o
   s o **K**
   It's O**K**.

4. da
   got a
   got a great **view**
   n it's got a great **view**
   An(d) it's got a great **view**.

5. zar
   windows are
   windows are there?
   How many **windows** are there?

6. kit
   like it.
   I **like** it.

4 PRACTICE

**Work with a partner. Describe one room in your apartment or house.
As you describe your room, your partner will draw it.**

EXAMPLE

There are two windows in the room.
Where are they?

5 EXCHANGE

Stand up. Walk around the room.
Ask about your classmates' rooms.

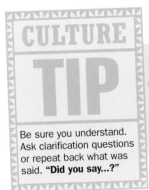
BASIC CONVERSATION

Tell me about your room.
OK.
Do you have any windows?
Yes, I have one. It's next to...

BONUS

Try to use some of these expressions.

ASKING
- Is it big or small?
- Where is it in your room?
- How many windows are there?
- Is it near (your door)?

TO CONFIRM THE INFORMATION
- Can you say that again?
- Do you mean (that it's near the window)?

ANSWERING
- I said that (the window is small).
- No, I meant that (the dresser is across from the window).

6 VOCABULARY BUILDING

Look at the illustration. Find these items:

a driveway, a garage, a fountain, a lawn, a garden, a hedge, a fence, a gate, a patio, a barbecue, some outdoor furniture, a chimney, some steps, a sidewalk, a mailbox, a balcony, a porch, a front door, a front yard

7 SMALL TALK: GILLIGAN'S ISLAND

Gilligan's Island was a popular comedy TV series in the U.S. during the 1960s. In this TV story, a group of people was shipwrecked in the South Pacific and had to live on a small tropical island. There were seven people on Gilligan's Island: Gilligan (a sailor), the Skipper (the captain of the ship), Mr. and Mrs. Howell (a rich tourist couple), Ginger (a movie star), Mary Ann (a young woman from a farm), and the Professor (a university professor). Each episode in the series was a story about the comic problems they had living together on the tiny island.

Talk about these questions with your classmates.

If you had to live with some people on an island for a year, who would you choose?

What 10 things would you bring with you to the island?

8 COMMUNICATION TASK — Design your own island

Work with a partner. Imagine that you are going to design your own island home. There will be four men and four women who will live on it.

What will you include? (Think about plants and animals, too.)
Make a sketch of your island home. Post your sketch in the classroom.

to include

-
-
-
-
-
-
-
-
-
-

9 GRAMMAR CHECK

Look back at the picture on page 40. Complete this paragraph with the correct prepositions.

in front of   across from   between   next to   in   behind   around   near   on

1. The patio is .... the house.

2. The car is .... the driveway, ... the garage.

3. The tree is .... the front yard, ... the steps and the mailbox.

4. There is a balcony .... the second floor.

5. There are some birds .... the fountain.

6. There is a garden .... the house.

7. The garage is .... the house.

8. There is a fence .... the patio.

41

9 Money

GRAMMAR TARGETS

Prices	How much	**does** it **cost?** **is** it?			It **costs** It's	99 dollars. ($99)
	How much	**do** they **cost?** **are they?**			They **cost** They're	5 dollars. ($5)
Opinions	I think She thinks	it's they're it's they're	a little too too kind of very	expensive. much. cheap. inexpensive.		
Advice	I **don't think**	I he	**should**	buy it.		
	He **thinks**	they we	**should**	get it.		

WARM UP   *What do you like spending money on? Think of five things.*
Example: travel

1 CONVERSATION 📟

Look at the picture. *Where are they? What is happening?*

Fill in the missing words. Then listen and check your answers.

Brian: Hey, this is a nice stereo.

Anna: Yes, it is nice. How much _____?
does it   is it

Brian: Ooh... _____ costs $1,200.
it's   it

Anna: Ouch! Brian, there's no way we can _____ this stereo.
afford   spend

Brian: Well, we could put _____ on our credit card.
it   them

Anna: No, I don't think that's a _____ idea.
bad   good

Brian: You're right.

Now practice the conversation.

2 LISTENING 📼

Listen and write the correct information.

    1. Debra's problem: ....

    2. Jack's goal: ....

3 PRONUNCIATION TIP 📼

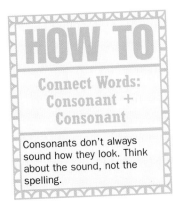

HOW TO

Connect Words:
Consonant +
Consonant

Consonants don't always sound how they look. Think about the sound, not the spelling.

If a word ends in the sounds f, v, l, m, n, ng, r, w, s, sh, th, z, ž...	**If a word ends in the sounds p, b, t, d, k, g...**
Go immediately into the next consonant sound. Don't pause! Keep your voice going.	Start the sound, but don't finish it. Hold your breath for a split second //. Then say the next consonant sound.
a ni**ce s**tereo	two hundre(**d**) // **d**ollars

Decide how to link the highlighted consonant sounds.

1. a credi**t c**ard
2. We coul**d p**ut it on our credi**t c**ard.
3. I don'**t think th**at's a good idea.
4. We ha**ve t**o wait.

5. a clothi**ng s**tore
6. a boo**k s**tore and a musi**c s**tore
7. Wha**t did th**ey ge**t th**ere?

Now listen and repeat. Speak as smoothly as possible.

4 PRACTICE

Work with a partner. Choose one of the stores below.
Ask your partner about shopping.

EXAMPLE

Which clothing store do you usually shop at?
I usually shop at Macy's.
What have you bought there recently?
I bought some shoes there last month.

electronic store
• computer • television
• stereo

furniture store
• chair • table • lamp

toy store
• jigsaw puzzle • board game • Nintendo game

Choose one more kind of store.

YOUR CHOICE •

music store
• CD • CD player • video

jewelry store
• ring • necklace • earrings

book store
• paperback • calendar
• book

clothing store
• shoes • pants • cosmetics

5 EXCHANGE

Stand up. Walk around the class.
Ask your classmates for advice about places to shop.

CULTURE TIP

It's best to give "soft" advice.
"I think...is a good place."
NOT
"You should go to..." or
"You'd better go to..."

BASIC CONVERSATION

Hey, _____. I wonder if you can help me.
    Sure, _____. What is it?
Where can I buy a _____?
    I think _____ is the best place.
OK. Thanks for your advice.

BONUS

Try to use some of these expressions.

ASKING FOR ADVICE
•Could I ask you for some advice?

ASKING ABOUT A PLACE
•Where's the best place to buy a...?
•What do you think is a good place
  to buy a...?
•Do you know anything about (place)?

GIVING ADVICE
•I think _____ is a good place.
•I don't think _____ is a good place.
•I think _____ is better than _____.

6 VOCABULARY BUILDING

Fill in the blanks in each sentence with the correct word.

1. (worth, cost) These shirts _____ $100 each! I don't think they're _____ that much.

2. (earn, save) I need to _____ a lot of money because I need to _____ for my college tuition.

3. (lease, buy) I wanted to _____ a new car, but I didn't have enough money. I had to _____ one instead.

4. (discount, bargain) This furniture was a _____. I got a _____ because my friend works at the store.

5. (exchange, return) I wanted to _____ this jacket, but the sales clerk said I could only _____ it for another one.

6. (write a check, pay cash) Jim didn't have any ID, so he couldn't _____. Instead he had to _____.

7 SMALL TALK: INTO THE WILD

In June 1990, Christopher Johnson graduated from a top university in Atlanta, Georgia. Christopher came from a wealthy family and was an excellent athlete and student. Most people thought that Christopher would become successful in business, just like his parents.

But Christopher had a different idea. Without telling his family, he took all of his money out of his bank account and gave it away. Then he took the money in his wallet and burned it.

Christopher decided to hitchhike to Alaska to live alone in the wild, with no money. He wanted to live his dream of being free.

You can read about Christopher's adventure in Jon Krakauer's book *Into the Wild*.

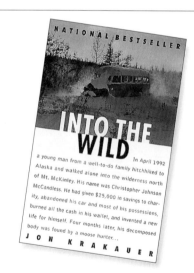

NATIONAL BESTSELLER

INTO THE WILD

a young man from a well-to-do family hitchhiked to Alaska and walked alone into the wilderness north of Mt. McKinley. His name was Christopher Johnson McCandless. He had given $25,000 in savings to charity, abandoned his car and most of his possessions, burned all the cash in his wallet, and invented a new life for himself. Four months later, his decomposed body was found by a moose hunter... In April 1992

JON KRAKAUER

Talk about these questions with your classmates.

Why did Christopher decide to give away his money?

Why did he decide to live "in the wild"? Do you think he was happy?

What do you think is the key to happiness?

8 COMMUNICATION TASK — *Ideas about money*

**Work with a partner. Here are some ideas about money.
What do these ideas mean to you?**

I'D LIKE TO LIVE LIKE
A POOR MAN WHO HAS
A LOT OF MONEY.

PABLO PICASSO

WHERE THERE IS
MONEY, THERE IS
GRIEF.

A PERSIAN PROVERB

A FOOL AND HIS
MONEY ARE
SOON PARTED.

AN ENGLISH PROVERB

YOU SHOULD NEVER
SPEND YOUR MONEY
BEFORE YOU'VE
EARNED IT.

A RUSSIAN PROVERB

MONEY
MAKES THE WORLD
GO AROUND.

A SONG LYRIC

COMMUNICATION
GOAL

*Which ideas are the
most useful?*

**Which ideas do you both agree with?
Write down two new sentences you both believe about money.**

* _____

* _____

Read your ideas to the class.

9 GRAMMAR CHECK

Match the sentences that have a similar meaning.

You shouldn't spend so much money.	That ring is too expensive for you.
You should wait until you can afford it.	I think I'll get this while it is discounted.
I think that this gold ring is better than that silver one.	I think you spent too much for that.
I think it's a little too expensive.	You shouldn't get it right now.
I think that is the best place for clothes.	I think you're spending too much money.
I think you can find a cheaper ring.	You should buy this gold ring.
I should charge this while it is on sale.	You should buy clothes there.
You shouldn't have spent so much for that.	I think that you need to use your credit card less.
I should stop spending money.	I think that I am spending too much lately.
I don't think you should charge so much.	I don't think it is cheap enough.

ACTIVITY 1   S P E A K I N G   C I R C L E S

CONJUNCTIONS	GRAMMAR TARGETS
And	I miss eating real Italian food, **and** I miss seeing my friends.
But	I miss my friends, **but** I don't miss the weather.
Or	I need to buy a new wallet, **or** I need to repair my old one.
Because	I want to move **because** my house is too small.
So	My house is too small, **so** I want to move.

❶ Sit in two rows. Face each other.
❷ Start with TOPIC 1.
❸ Talk to your partner for 1 minute.
❹ Then change partners.
❺ Talk for 1 minute about the same topic.
❻ Continue for 3 or 4 partners.
❼ Start again on TOPIC 2 with a new partner.

CONVERSATION

TIP

Don't be embarrassed
to ask questions.

TOPIC 1

PERSONAL ITEMS

Sample questions:
Is your watch round or square?
What's the most important thing you own?
Do you lose things very often?
What things do you usually carry with you?

TOPIC 2

ENTERTAINMENT

Sample questions:
Where's your favorite place to meet friends?
Why do you like to go there?
Do you know a good place to meet
English speakers?
How many times do you eat out in a month?

TOPIC 4

NATIONALITY

Sample questions:
Where were you born?
What do you miss about your hometown?
Could you move to another country
and live there forever?
What would you miss about this country?

TOPIC 3

HOME

Sample questions:
What's your home like?
Do you live alone or with people?
Can you describe one room in your house?
What would your perfect home be like?

TOPIC 5

MONEY

Sample questions:
Do you like to go shopping?
Where do you usually shop?
Where's the best place to buy English books?
Is having a lot of money important to you?

ACTIVITY 2 ROLE PLAY

Work with a partner. Choose a situation. Make up a dialogue.
Practice your dialogue. Then say your dialogue in front of the class.

EXAMPLE

Two classmates talk about their background.

Lance: Were you born here?
Truyen: *No, but I have lived here since I was 10.*
Lance: Where did you live before that?
Truyen: *Vietnam. I was born there.*

CULTURE TIP

Don't be shy. Try out your dialogue in front of the class.

SITUATION 1

A woman is describing her Christmas presents to a friend.

Possible Expressions:

My boyfriend gave me a _____ and a _____.

Did he get them because you asked him to?

What kind of _____ did he get you?

It's green and yellow, but I don't like it.

SITUATION 2

Two people are making plans for Saturday night.

Possible Expressions:

Would you like to go to a movie or a play?

Let's go to dinner and a concert.

I don't want to do that because I'm on a diet.

What's a good but cheap restaurant?

SITUATION 3

A couple is shopping for a new car.

Possible Expressions:

Don't you think it's too expensive?

This one is better because it has four doors.

We can get that one, but we will need a loan.

Do you know anything about this model of car?

SITUATION 4

A person is trying to cheer up a homesick friend.

Possible Expressions:

Today is my dad's birthday, so I'm sad.

Tell me about your dad.

I know you miss your family, but you have many friends here.

What do you miss the most about your country?

SITUATION 5

A person is describing her new apartment to a friend.

Possible Expressions:

What's your new apartment like?

Which do you like better: your new place or your old one?

It's nice and big.

In the living room, there's a white sofa across from the TV.

10 Personality

GRAMMAR TARGETS

Asking about people	What	**do**	you they	**think of**	him? us?	I They	think	he's we're	smart. nice.
	What	**does**	she he	**think of**	me? her?	She He	thinks	you're she's	funny. boring.
Descriptions	She He They	's looks seem	**a little** shy. **a bit** mean. **really** nice.						
Getting More Information	Why do you		say **that**? think **so**?			She They	**never** **always**	talks help	to me. me

WARM UP   *Who is someone you would like to meet? Why?*

1 CONVERSATION

Look at the picture. *Where are they? What's happening?*

Fill in the missing words. Then listen and check your answers.

Alex: _____ met Gill Brady?

Do you ever   Have you ever

Debbie: Oh, sure. _____

I know   I've known

her for a long time.

Alex: What _____ you

did   do

think of her?

Debbie: Well, she's one of the most

_____ people I've ever met.

fascinated   fascinating

Alex: Really? What makes you

_____ that?

say   tell

Debbie: I don't know. She always
has something interesting

_____ about.

talking   to talk

Alex: Hmm. I think she is

_____ self-centered.

too   such

Now practice the conversation.

2 LISTENING 📟

Listen and write the correct information. How do they describe the people?

1. Tony: ....

2. Tanya: ....

3 PRONUNCIATION TIP 📟

HOW TO

**Connect Words:
Consonant +
dropped "h" and "th"**

You'll understand spoken English more easily if you learn to drop /h/ and /th/ in personal pronouns. You'll sound better, too!

You can drop /h/ and /th/ in *he, him, his, her* and *them* when these words are:
• unstressed
• in the middle of a phrase
• at the end of a sentence

Make these words very weak:
he   → /i/
him → /ɪm/ or /əm/
his → /əz/
her → /ər/
them → /əm/ or /ðəm/

Listen and repeat.

1. f her
   k of her
   think of her
   What do you **think** of her?

2. n her
   known her
   known her a
   known her a long **time**
   I've known her a long **time**.

3. f them
   n of them
   rimpression of them
   your **impression** of them
   What's your **impression** of them?

4. t his
   met his
   met his **family**
   Have you met his **family**?

4 PRACTICE

Work with a partner. Look at each picture. What is your impression of each person?

EXAMPLE

What do you think of her?
She looks...
She seems...

49

5 EXCHANGE

Stand up. Talk to your classmates.
Ask about their impressions of each person in Activity 4.

BONUS
Try to use some of these expressions.

COMMUNICATION TIP

Use modifiers to make your opinions clearer.

It's ...	...sort of...
a little...	really...
a bit...	very...
somewhat...	completely...

BASIC CONVERSATION

What do you think of #1?
I think he's sort of...
Why do you think so?

ASKING
- What makes you say that?
- Why do you say that?

ANSWERING
- He seems a bit _____.
- I don't like the way she looks.

AGREEING
- I think so, too.
- I don't think so, either.
- Me, too.
- Me neither.

DISAGREEING
- Well, I think she's _____.
- Do you really think she's _____?

6 VOCABULARY BUILDING

Work with a partner.
Can you think of another way to say the following sentences?

1. He's romantic. _____
2. She's straightforward. _____
3. He's goofy. _____
4. She's open-minded. _____
5. He's sharp. _____

6. She's sensitive. _____
7. He's witty. _____
8. She's strong-willed. _____
9. He's fun. _____
10. She's understanding. _____

7 SMALL TALK: CLIMATE AND EMOTIONS

Do you believe this stereotype? People from warm climates are emotionally "expressive," while people from cold climates are emotionally "reserved."

According to *Psychology Today* magazine, it turns out, on average, that people in warmer climates actually do rate their expressiveness slightly higher than people who live in colder climates. People who live in the warmer parts of their country say they are "more expressive" and find it easier to "show their emotions." People who live in the colder parts of their country admit they are more "constrained" and find it less comfortable to show their feelings.

What's the reason? Cold weather constrains your ability to express emotion. In colder climates, people tend to spend more time indoors, wear more clothes, and be less physical — all of which make us less expressive.

Talk about these questions with your classmates.

Are people from the warmer parts of your country more expressive?

How are people in the different parts of your country different?

Why are some people more expressive than others?

8 COMMUNICATION TASK  *Impressions*

Work in a group of 4. Write down the names of 5 famous people that all of you know.

an old woman

What is she like?

....

facts or examples

....

an old man

What is he like?

....

facts or examples

....

a child

What is he/she like?

....

facts or examples

....

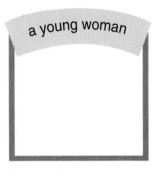

a young woman

What is she like?

....

facts or examples

....

a young man

What is he like?

....

facts or examples

....

COMMUNICATION

GOAL

What did you learn about these people?

•

What is each person like? Share your impressions of each person with the group.
Give a fact or an example to show what you mean.

9 GRAMMAR CHECK

Match each question with the best answer.

Does she usually talk so much?
What's your impression of Sid and Nancy?
What do you think of her?
Have you met Susan before?
Why do you think she's shy?
What's he like?
Do you think Ed is funny?
What makes you say Brenda's boring?
Do you really thing they're mean?
What does Bill think of us?

Yes, we met at Jack's party.
Well, she just never says anything interesting.
He thinks we are snobby.
Yes, they always make me mad.
He's nice.
She seems very sweet.
Yes, he always makes me laugh.
Yes, she's very outgoing.
Because she never talks to me.
They seem a little wild to me.

Now practice the conversations with a partner.

11 Around Town

GRAMMAR TARGETS

Asking for Directions	Where is	**the** bus stop? Macy's Department Store?		
	Where's	**the** 42nd Street subway station? Madison Avenue?		
Indirect Questions	Do you know	**where**	the 42nd Street bus station Macy's Department Store	**is**?
Locations	The bus stop Macy's The theater It's	is	**on** **near** **next to** **across from**	First Street. the bus station. the post office. the bank.
Giving Directions	Turn right Go straight Turn left	**on** Maple Drive **for** 2 kilometers. **at** the post office	and then	**walk** 200 meters. **turn** left at the church. **go** to the next corner.

WARM UP *Name five places in town that you go to often.*

1 CONVERSATION

Look at the picture. *Where are they? What is happening?*

Fill in the missing words. Then listen and check your answers.

Simon: Excuse me.

Penny: Yes?

Simon: I'm trying to _____ Civic Station.
get   find

Penny: Civic? I'm _____ not   no
sure, but I think it's that way.

Simon: _____ way?
What   Which

Penny: That way. Toward Market Street. I think it's _____
near   close
Market Street.

Simon: OK. Thanks for your
_____ .
help   helping

Penny: _____ .
Sure   Yes
No problem.

Now practice the conversation.

2 LISTENING

Listen and mark the correct place on the map.

1. The Tower Building

ROSE STREET
FIFTH AVENUE
FOURTH AVENUE
● You are here.

2. Matt's house

CALDWELL STREET
MAIN STREET
GREEN STREET ● You are here.

3 PRONUNCIATION TIP

HOW TO

Say the Names of Places

Be careful with names of places. Different types of place names have different types of stress patterns.

Street Names	**Other Street Names**	**Place Names**
Stress the name of the street. Keep "street" low:	Stress the last word. Keep the name low:	Stress the last word of the name:
Market Street	Madison **Avenue**	Civic **Station**

For other types of compound nouns, stress the first word:
post office, **subway** station, **bus** stop

Listen and underline the stressed words.

1. 42nd Street
2. Central Park
3. Sumitomo Bank
4. First Street
5. Maple Drive
6. Green Street
7. Green Station
8. Redwood Park
9. 7-Eleven
10. Circle K

Listen again and repeat.

4 PRACTICE

Work with a partner. Look at the map. Can you tell how to get to each place?

EXAMPLE

Where is 7-Eleven?
It's on Second Street.
Go straight to Second Street.
Then turn left.

5 EXCHANGE

Draw a map of the area near your school.
Mark three places you like to go to.
Now stand up and talk to your classmates.
Give directions to your three places.

BASIC CONVERSATION

Do you know where _____ is?
No, I'm not sure. Where is it?
You just go...

BONUS

Try to use some of these expressions.

GIVING DIRECTIONS
- It's not far from here.
- You can't miss it.
- When you leave the school, go north.
- Walk for about (1 minute/100 meters).

HELPING
- Do you know (Macy's)? It's near that.

FINISHING UP
- OK. I think I can find it.
- You've been a big help, thanks.

6 VOCABULARY BUILDING

Work with a partner.
Find these places on the map.

1. It's across from Ala Moana Shopping Center.
2. It's an old volcano. You can see it easily from Waikiki Beach.
3. It's a hotel that's located right on Waikiki Beach.
4. It's along University Avenue, not far from King Street.
5. It's a large area, located near where Highway 1 and the Pali Highway cross.
6. It's a big building, on the corner of Bishop Street and King Street.
7. It's not far from Waikiki Beach. It's along the canal.

Now cover the sentences.
Can you describe where each place is?

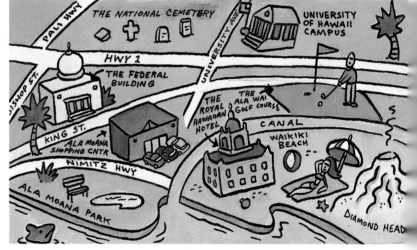

7 SMALL TALK: UNUSUAL ENTERTAINMENT SPOTS

The Blake Street Baseball Club, in Denver, Colorado, is an unusual kind of place. This "sports bar" is located in the oldest part of the city. It's designed to look like a baseball stadium. It has natural grass as floors and no roof. The dance floor is called "Center Field." It's open only during the summer because it's cold in Denver during the winter. It's usually very crowded, especially when a local baseball game is on TV.

Talk about these questions with your classmates.

What is your favorite entertainment spot in your city? Is it unusual in any way?

What is the most unusual entertainment spot you know?

What would you do to make an entertainment spot unusual?

8 COMMUNICATION TASK — *Places in the city*

Choose one of these topics:

THE MOST POPULAR MEETING PLACE

THE BEST PARK

THE MOST INTERESTING RESTAURANT

THE BEST COFFEE SHOP

THE QUIETEST PLACE

THE BEST MUSIC STORE

COMMUNICATION **GOAL**

Which new places would you like to go to?

SUNRISE CAFÉ

Write two or three key ideas about your topic:

key word   key word   key word

Work in a group of 4.
Try to talk for one minute about your topic.

"I'm going to talk about…"
"It's interesting because…"

At the end of your "speech," ask: "Any questions?"

9 GRAMMAR CHECK

Each conversation has one or two errors. Find the errors and correct them.

1. Where is the bus stop?
   It's in front ^of^ Stewart's department store.

2. Do you know where is the station?
   It's over there.

3. Is there a post office near to here?
   Yes, there's a post office on Civic Street.

4. Where's Sutton Street?
   Turn right the bus station.

5. Excuse me. I trying find Market Street.
   This is Market Street!

6. Is the Apex Theatre is near here?
   Yes, just walk about 100 meters.

7. Is Sumitomo Bank on this street?
   No, it isn't. It the next street.

8. Go to First Street and turn the right.
   Thank. I think I can find it.

9. Do you know where Kirin City is?
   I'm not sure. Is near the train station?

10. Excuse me. I'm finding the City Hall.
    I'm not sure. Maybe you should ask someone else.

Now practice the corrected conversation.

12 Daily Schedule

UNIT

WARM UP *What are four things that you do every day?*

1 CONVERSATION 📼

Look at the picture. *Where are they? What is happening?*

Fill in the missing words. Then listen and check your answers.

Tracy: That was a great movie, but I should _____ soon. Do
    be go   be going
you know what time _____?
               it is   is it

Randy: Let me check. It's _____
                       about   close
10:45.

Tracy: 10:45? The last train
_____ at 11, doesn't it?
leaves   left

Randy: Yeah, I _____.
              think so   know

Tracy: Gosh, I've _____
                   got to   have to
run. If I miss the train, I'll have to
take a taxi.

Randy: OK. See you _____.
                    after   later

Tracy: Bye. Thanks for _____
                         invite   inviting
me over.

Now practice the conversation.

56

2 LISTENING 📼

Listen and write the correct information. What time is it? Why do they have to hurry?

1. Elaine
   Time: ....
   Reason to hurry: ....

2. Bob
   Time: ....
   Reason to hurry: ....

3 PRONUNCIATION TIP 📼

<table>
<tr><td align="center">On the Hour</td><td align="center">After the Hour</td></tr>
<tr><td>

"It's 11 o'clock."
• Stress "clock".
• Reduce "o" to / ə /.
• Connect the words.
  It's_eleven_ə**clock**

"It's 11." (It's 11:00.)
• Stress the number. Connect the words:
  It's_**eleven**. Or add "o'clock".
  It's_elevən_əclock.

</td><td>

"It's 10:05."
• Stress the last number.
• Say the letter "O" for the minutes
  :01 through :09.
• Connect the numbers.
  It's ten_"O"_**five**.

</td></tr>
</table>

HOW TO
Stress Numbers When Telling the Time

Use stress and linking to help you tell the time. Sometimes what we write isn't what we say.

Listen. Write the times. Then repeat.

1. The last train leaves at ....
2. I get up around ....
3. It's almost ....
4. I've got to be somewhere at ....
5. The bus gets here at ....

4 PRACTICE

Work with a partner. Ask about your partner's daily schedule.

| 1. What time do you usually get up? | 2. What time do you usually get to work (or school)? | 3. How long does it take you to get there? | 4. When do you usually get home? | 5. How much time do you usually spend getting ready for work or school? | 6. How much time do you usually spend at home? | 7. How much time do you spend studying? |

Now think of two more questions to ask your partner:

• How much time do you spend .... ?

• How much time do you spend .... ?

57

5 EXCHANGE

Stand up. Ask your classmates about their schedules.

CULTURE TIP

Don't be afraid to introduce a new topic. **"Can I ask you some questions about...?"**

BASIC CONVERSATION

How much time do you usually sleep a night?
I guess I sleep about 7 hours a night. How about you? What time do you ...?

BONUS

Try to use some of these expressions.

STARTING
• Do you mind if I ask you some questions?
• Go ahead.

ASKING
• How long does it take you to _____?

SHOWING SURPRISE
• No way! You sleep only 3 hours a night?
• You're kidding! A 6-hour commute?

6 VOCABULARY BUILDING

How long do you spend on each activity every day?

_____ talking on the phone
_____ brushing your teeth
_____ taking a bath or shower
_____ listening to the radio
_____ doing your English homework

_____ reading and answering your mail
_____ getting ready for school or work
_____ commuting to school or work
_____ cleaning up your house
_____ making food

_____ reading for fun
_____ sleeping
_____ washing dishes
_____ watching TV
_____ visiting with friends

Now compare your answers with a partner.

7 SMALL TALK: STRESS TEST

Most people today have too much stress in their lives. Some stress makes us active and creative, but too much stress is bad for our health. Which areas of your life cause you the most stress?

	very little stress	some stress	a lot of stress
HOME LIFE			
HEALTH			
MONEY			
JOB			
LOVE LIFE			
DAILY SCHEDULE			
PARENTS			
NEIGHBORS			
CITY LIFE			
COMMUTING			
STUDYING ENGLISH			

Talk about these questions with your classmates.

What causes you the most stress? (school, job, family)

What is one way you could cut down the stress in your life?

8 COMMUNICATION TASK

Work with a partner. Which of these activities help you relax?

	This usually helps me relax.	This sometimes helps me relax.	This doesn't help me relax.	I've never tried it.
RELAXING ACTIVITIES listening to music				
reading				
watching TV				
eating a special food				
yoga				
relaxation exercises				
running or exercising				
meditating				
talking to close friends				
playing with my pet				
taking care of my garden				
drinking alcohol				
drinking coffee				
taking a nap				
taking a hot bath				
getting a massage				
other:				

COMMUNICATION GOAL

Which activities would you like to try?

●

Compare your answers. Which activities do you both enjoy?

9 GRAMMAR CHECK

Make sentences with the words given. There is one extra word in each line.

1. you   cooking   how   long   spend   to   do   dinner

   ....?

2. What   it   time   is   that

   ....?

3. to   have   somewhere   5:30   I've   be   at   got

   ....

4. school   take   get   you   to   does   to   often   long   how   it

   ....?

5. Erin   an   spends   playing   hour   computer   usually   games   spend

   ....

6. much   your   time   spend   up   you   many   cleaning   how   do   house

   ....?

7. mind   do   I   questions   me   if   you   ask   you   some

   ....?

8. It's   seven   nearly   o'clock   mostly

   ....

9. get   school   time   you   use   do   to   what   usually

   ....

10. Sue   go   Dave   work   and   9 o'clock   to   at   works

   ....

13 Modern Life

UNIT

GRAMMAR TARGETS

Instructions	The phone The modem	has to **be**	plugg**ed** in. turn**ed** on.	
	The wires	have to **be**	connect**ed**.	
	You He	have to has to	**plug** it in. **turn** it on.	
Naming	**What's the name** of **What do you call**	that machine the machine	used to videotape people? over there?	It's a camcorder. It's called a joy stick.
Use	What is **that used** for? What do you **use it** for?	You **use it** **It's used**	for	look**ing** up words. talk**ing** to people.

WARM UP ***What three machines do you use every day?***

1 CONVERSATION

Look at the picture. ***Where are they? What's happening?***

Fill in the missing words. Then listen and check your answers.

Robert: What's ____________?
wrong problem

Dennis: I can't get this modem to ____________, and I need to
work do
check my e-mail.

Robert: Let me ____________.
watch see
Oh, the telephone line has to ____________ in.
plug be plugged

Dennis: Oh, gosh. Stupid ________!
me you
It's a good thing you were here.

Robert: Don't feel bad. A ________
lots lot
of people ____________ that mistake.
do make

Now practice the conversation.

2 LISTENING

Listen and write the correct information. What machine are they talking about?
What did they forget to do?

1. Dale

   Machine: ....

   Forgot to: ....

2. Ms. Miller

   Machine: ....

   Forgot to: ....

3 PRONUNCIATION TIP

HOW TO

Reduce "has to" and "have to"

In conversation, "has to" and "have to" sound like *"hasta"* and *"hafta"* because they have weak stress. Use these reductions in normal, natural, relaxed conversation. Keep them low, weak, and unstressed.

has to
1. Stress the most important words.
The **telephone** line *hæstə* be **plugged in**.
2. Say "hasta" for "has to".

have to
1. Stress the most important words.
You *hæftə* **plug** it **in**.
2. Say "hafta" for "have to".

Listen. You will hear some sentences with careful pronunciation, then relaxed pronunciation.
Repeat them with relaxed pronunciation. Use *"hasta"* and *"hafta"*.

1. You _____ plug it in.
2. It _____ be plugged in.
3. You _____ turn it on.
4. It _____ be turned on.
5. The modem _____ be plugged in.
6. The lights _____ be turned on.

*Use "has to" and "have to" when you write.

4 PRACTICE

Work with a partner. Look at each item. Do you have one? Do you use one often?

EXAMPLE

Do you have a _____?
Yes, I do.
Do you use it often?

copy machine, refrigerator, air freshener, electronic dictionary, calculator, air conditioner, Walkman®, electric razor, cellular phone, scanner, pager, massage chair, television, Discman, radio, cassette player, CD player, electric fan, remote control for the TV

Can you think of two other "modern" machines?

-
-

5 EXCHANGE

Walk around the class.
Play this guessing game with your classmates. Ask "What's the name of the machine that is used to ...?"

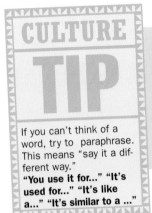

BASIC CONVERSATION

What's the matter?
I can't think of the name of the machine that people use to call each other.
It's called a telephone.
Oh, right. Thanks!

BONUS

Try to use some of these expressions.

ASKING IF YOU CAN HELP
• You look worried. Can I help you ?
• Can I do something for you?

ASKING
• Can you help me out?
• What's the name of the thing that you use to...?
• Do you know what machine I am talking about?

ANSWERING
• Yes, it's a ...
• Sorry, I don't know what that's called.
• Maybe you should ask (name)...

6 VOCABULARY BUILDING

Fill in the correct particle in each sentence.
Example: Please pick up your shoes.

down   away   up   down   in   down   on   off   in   with

1. Pour the water _____ the pan.
2. Fill the pan _____ water.
3. Hold _____ the mouse button on your computer.
4. Turn _____ the TV if you want to watch it.
5. I'm going to bed. Would you turn _____ the TV, please?
6. You need to shut _____ the computer when you are done.

7. You never put _____ your books when you're finished with them.
8. Dinner will be ready as soon as I heat _____ the soup.
9. The tea will cool _____ if you put it in the refrigerator.
10. Plug _____ the printer cord.

7 SMALL TALK: MODERN INVENTIONS

Every year there are countless new inventions to "improve our life." Here are two examples from inventor Bryan Mumford.

The Frog Rock

This is a natural sandstone boulder that seems to float a little above the floor. Inside the stone, there is a processor that has digitally recorded sounds of insects (like crickets) and amphibians (like frogs). The sounds play according to a 24-hour cycle, giving the listener an experience of being in nature. "This allows people to bring wildlife into their homes," says the inventor.

The Shirtpocket Billboard

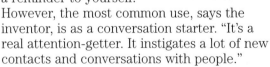

This is a small, battery-operated computer with a small display screen. It fits into your shirt or jacket pocket, with the display screen sticking out of your pocket. You can program a message to play constantly, as a reminder to yourself.
However, the most common use, says the inventor, is as a conversation starter. "It's a real attention-getter. It instigates a lot of new contacts and conversations with people."

Talk about these questions with your classmates.

What useful inventions do you use often?

What new invention would you design to improve our life?

8 COMMUNICATION TASK — *Dream Machine*

Work with a partner. Think of one invention idea for each topic.

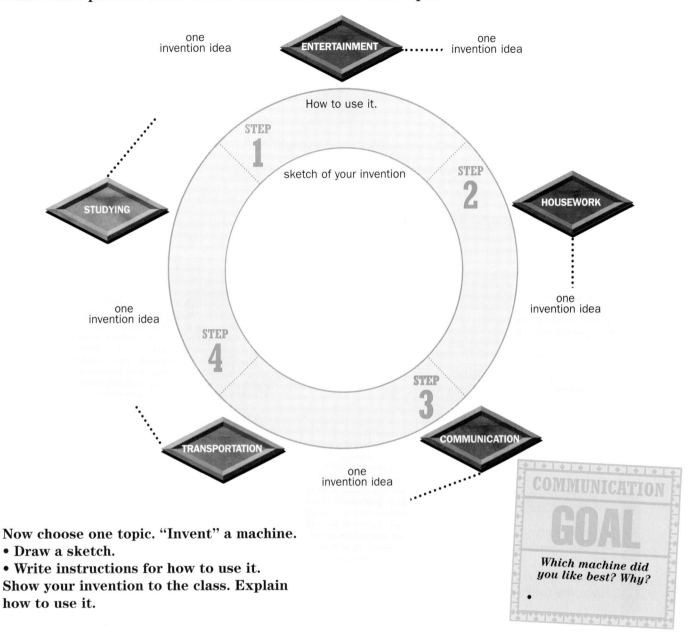

Now choose one topic. "Invent" a machine.
- **Draw a sketch.**
- **Write instructions for how to use it.**

Show your invention to the class. Explain how to use it.

COMMUNICATION GOAL

Which machine did you like best? Why?

-

9 GRAMMAR CHECK

Each conversation has one or two errors. Correct the errors.

1. What's wrong?

   I can't get this modem work.

2. Let me seeing.

   Do you know what wrong?

3. Yes, the telephone line has to be plug in.

   Oh, you're right. I forgot do that.

4. Do you know the name of the machine that you use to scan pictures?

   Yes, that called a "scanner."

5. Do you know how using it?

   Yes, you just put a picture on the glass.

Now practice the conversations with a partner.

ACTIVITY 1 SPEAKING CIRCLES

CONJUNCTIONS	GRAMMAR TARGETS
But	I don't remember her last name, **but** I do remember her first name.
Because	She seems friendly **because** she always talks to everyone.
Since	He looks a bit wild **since** he has a pierced nose and tongue.
Even though	We decided to go to the museum **even though** it was already 4 o'clock.
Although	**Although** I work at home, I am very busy during the day.

❶ Sit in two rows. Face each other.
❷ Start with TOPIC 1.
❸ Talk to your partner for 1 minute.
❹ Then change partners.
❺ Talk for 1 minute about the same topic.
❻ Continue for 3 or 4 partners.
❼ Start again on TOPIC 2 with a new partner.

CONVERSATION TIP

Don't be embarrassed to ask questions.

PERSONAL IMPRESSIONS

TOPIC 1

Sample questions:
What do you think of our teacher?
Why do you think that?
Who is the strangest person you know?
Have you ever met a famous person?

AROUND TOWN

TOPIC 2

Sample questions:
Can you give me directions to your house?
Where is your favorite restaurant?
What cities can you get around in without a map?
When was the last time you got lost?

DAILY SCHEDULE

TOPIC 3

Sample questions:
What is your normal daily schedule?
How much time do you spend watching TV a day?
What would be your perfect daily schedule?
How long does it take you to get to class?

MODERN LIFE

TOPIC 4

Sample questions:
What's the newest machine you have?
Do you like computers or are you scared of them?
Do you think young children should have a computer to do their homework on?
Are there any machines that you can't use although you would like to?

ACTIVITY 2 ROLE PLAY

Work with a partner. Choose a situation. Make up a dialogue.
Practice your dialogue. Then say your dialogue in front of the class.

EXAMPLE

A woman is looking for the train station.

Ann: Do you know where the station is?
Tony: *I'm not sure, but I think it's on Scott Street.*
Ann: Scott?
Tony: *Yeah, at the corner turn right and walk 2 more blocks.*

SITUATION 1

Two co-workers are trying to fix a computer.

Possible Expressions:

Can I help you with anything?

What is that cord used for?

Maybe you should call someone since we can't make it work.

I think you need to plug that cord into the back of the computer.

SITUATION 2

Two lost people are looking for their hotel.

Possible Expressions:

Where's the hotel we are staying at?

Should we ask someone where it is?

Even though the man said to turn right, I think we should go left.

The man said that it was close to the park.

SITUATION 3

Two friends who haven't seen each other in years meet.

Possible Expressions:

How much time do you spend with your kids?

What time do you usually get home at night?

I am very busy because I just started a new job.

I'd like to talk more, but I've got to run. I'm late for work.

SITUATION 4

A couple is talking with another couple they have just met.

Possible Expressions:

What do you think of them?

What makes you say that?

Although I really liked him, I thought she was weird.

Do you think we should meet them again?

CULTURE TIP

Make eye contact with your partner when you speak.

GRAMMAR TARGETS

Destinations	Where	**are**	you they	**going**?		I'm They**'re**	**going to**	Hawaii. Taiwan.
	Where	**is**	she he	**going**?		She**'s** He**'s**		
Future Actions	What	**are** **is**	you he	going **to do**?		I'm He's	**going to**	**relax**. **work**.
	What	**do**	you they	**want to do**? **need to do**?		I They	**want to** **need to**	**go** hiking. **visit** his aunt.
	What	**does**	he she	**plan to do**? **hope to do**?		He She	**plans to** **hopes to**	**go** diving. **see** a whale.
Relative Clauses	Hawaii is **a place**			**that**	**has** nice beaches.			
	Canada is **a place**			**that**	**has** great ski resorts.			

WARM UP *What are your favorite places to take a vacation?*

1 CONVERSATION

Look at the picture. *Where are they? What is happening?*

Fill in the missing words. Then listen and check your answers.

Sue: Where are you and Jill _____ on your honeymoon?
<u>going   to go</u>

Jim: We're going to spend a week _____ Hawaii.
<u>at   in</u>

Sue: Oh, are you going _____
<u>in   to</u>
Maui or Oahu?

Jim: _____. We're going to Kauai.
<u>Neither   None</u>

Sue: Kauai? Where's _____?
<u>there   that</u>

Jim: It's one of the islands, to the north.

Sue: Oh, right. What are you going to do _____?
<u>there   here</u>

Jim: Nothing, really. We just want to _____. Planning this
<u>relax   relaxing</u>
wedding _____ stressful.
<u>is   has been</u>

Now practice the conversation.

66

2 LISTENING

Listen and write the correct information. Where are they going? What are they going to do there?

1. Bob: Place: _____
   Activity: _____

2. Katherine: Place: _____
   Activity: _____

3 PRONUNCIATION TIP

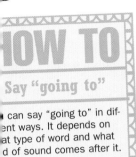

HOW TO

Say "going to"

You can say "going to" in different ways. It depends on what type of word and what kind of sound comes after it.

going to + place

1. Say "goingdə" Make it weak.

We're go ing də Ha wai i

2. Stress the most important word. We're goingdə **Hawaii**.

3. Say **ng** when you say "goingdə". Keep the tip of your tongue down. Hold the back of your tongue up. Send the air out of your nose.

going to + verb

1. Say "gonna" (gənə). Make it weak.

We're gə nə re L A X

2. Stress the most important word. We're gənə **relax**.

Listen. Check (✔) the phrase you hear. Mark the stressed syllables.

goingdə gənə
- ❏ ❏ 1. Are you going to Maui?
- ❏ ❏ 2. What are you going to do there?
- ❏ ❏ 3. We're going to spend a week in Hawaii.
- ❏ ❏ 4. He's going to Kauai.

goingdə gənə
- ❏ ❏ 5. He's going to go to Kauai.
- ❏ ❏ 6. They're going to swim.
- ❏ ❏ 7. She's going to a nice island.

Listen again and repeat.

4 PRACTICE

Work with a partner. Ask about vacation places that your partner knows.

EXAMPLE

What is a place that has nice beaches?
Kauai is a place that has nice beaches.

lots of shopping

exciting night spots

old buildings

fun music clubs

great scuba diving

good food

5 EXCHANGE

**Stand up. Walk around the class.
Ask your classmates for advice.**

**Don't be shy about starting a conversation.
Use a conversation opener. "I'd like to ask you something."**

BASIC CONVERSATION

Do you know a good _____?
  *Well, it depends on what you
  want to do there.*
I'm looking for somewhere that has _____.
  Oh, then I'd recommend _____.
              OR
  Oh, sorry, I can't think of any place.

BONUS

Try to use some of these expressions.

ASKING
• I want to go scuba diving. Do you
  know a good place?

ANSWERING
• That depends. How much do you want
  to spend?
• I know two good places. What
  specifically are you looking for?

GETTING MORE DETAILS
• That sounds nice. Is it expensive?
• Do you know how to get there?

6 VOCABULARY BUILDING

Work with a partner. Make 5 sentences about famous places.

Here are some ideas:

beaches	old buildings
art museums	electronics stores
canals	wonderful food
music clubs	castles
narrow streets	shopping districts

EXAMPLE

_____ is known for its _____.

In _____, you can visit some famous _____.

- ....
- ....
- ....
- ....
- ....

7 SMALL TALK: UNUSUAL VACATIONS

Some people don't like popular vacation spots. They want to do something that is a bit unusual.
Here is one unusual vacation idea.

International Expeditions offers frequent seven-
day trips to the jungles of the world: Peru, Uganda,
Indonesia, and other seldom-visited places. Each
trip is conducted by a naturalist who is an expert
on the geography and the animal and plant life of
the area. These expedition vacations are much
cheaper than four or five days in Honolulu!

Talk about these questions with your classmates.

*Would you be
interested in this type
of vacation idea?
Why or why not?*

*What is the most
unusual vacation you
have had?*

8 COMMUNICATION TASK

Work with a partner. Pretend you are tour guides for a group of tourists coming to your country for a one-week trip. Plan some activities for them.

First, decide:

What is the nationality of the group?	How old are they?
How many people are in the group?	How much money will they spend?

Think of several activities and several places to visit.

Examples:

exploring	swimming	visiting famous places
mountain climbing	hiking	shopping
going to museums	skiing	surfing
	scuba diving	

Draw a map and indicate the activities you recommend.
Present your plan to the class.

COMMUNICATION
GOAL

What new vacation ideas did you learn about?

•

9 GRAMMAR CHECK

Make sentences with the words given.

1. Kyoto   beautiful   place   is   a   that   has   lot   a   temples   of   .

2. where   going   they   are   for   vacation   their   ?

3. Kyoto   old   known   is   for   its   temples   .

4. what   do   going   you   husband   and   in   are   your   to   France   ?

5. small   in   we   southern   plan   to   visit   villages   some   France   .

6. stay   we   where   in   Pusan   should   we're   when   ?

7. think   Hilton   the   stay   should   you   I   at   Hotel   .

8. spend   in   going   Montreal   a   week   we're   to   .

9. a   can   visit   in   clubs   New York   you   dance   lot   of   .

10. New York   to   me   you   to   like   would   with   go   ?

Now make conversations using these sentences.

GRAMMAR TARGETS

Opinions							
	What do you **think of**	New York? living in Orlando? the traffic in Tokyo?		It's	**a little** **sort of** **kind of**	crowded. boring. annoying.	
	Which do you **like**	**better,** **more,**	Chicago Sidney	**or**	New York? Melbourne?		
	I like	Chicago Melbourne	**more than** **better than**	New York. Sidney.			
Comparisons	Portland is It's It **isn't**	ni**cer** **less** crowded **as** crowded	**than** **than** **as**	Chicago. Los Angeles. Tokyo.			

WARM UP *What are your favorite cities?*

1 CONVERSATION

Look at the picture. *Where are they? What is happening?*

Fill in the missing words. Then listen and check your answers.

Sachiko: _____ here
<small>You're living   You've lived</small>
for two months, right?

David: Yes, that's right. Just about two months.

Sachiko: What do you think of
_____ in Tokyo?
<small>live   living</small>

David: Oh, it's a _____
<small>sort of   little</small>
difficult, but I'm _____ used to it.
<small>get   getting</small>

Sachiko: If you _____ mind my
<small>don't   do</small>
asking, what's difficult about it?

David: Well, it's a little too
_____ for me.
<small>crowd   crowded</small>

Sachiko: Yeah, I know
_____. But don't worry.
<small>you mean that   what you mean</small>
You'll get _____ it soon.
<small>using to   used to</small>

Now practice the conversation.

2 LISTENING

Listen and write the correct information. What city are they talking about? What is their opinion?

1. Nina:

   City: ....

   Opinion: ....

2. Natalie:

   City: ....

   Opinion: ....

3 PRONUNCIATION TIP

HOW TO

Say /ər/ in Comparisons

Reduced sounds are important in fluent English pronunciation. We say these sounds quickly and quietly.

/ər/

1. Bring the tip of your tongue backward into your mouth.
2. Don't let the tip touch anything!
3. Keep your lips still and relaxed.

Repeat: /ər/   /ər/   /ər/
Now make /ər/ quick and quiet. Repeat: /ər/   /ər/   /ər/

Listen and repeat.

1. gər
   bigger
   bigger thən
   bigger thən New **York**.
   It's **bi**gger thən New **York**.

2. sər
   nicer
   nicer thən
   nicer thən **Hong** Kong.
   It's **ni**cer thən **Hong** Kong.

3. yər
   higher
   higher thən
   higher thən **Chicago**
   living is **high**er thən **Chicago**.
   The cost of **living** is **high**er thən **Chicago**.

4. ər
   moər
   moər crowded
   moər crowded thən
   moər crowded thən **Tokyo**
   It's moər crowded thən **Tokyo**.

4 PRACTICE

Work with a partner. Write the names of eight cities in your country.
Now take turns. Point to two cities in the grid. Make comparative statements.
Example: X is more _____ than Y.

5 EXCHANGE

Stand up. Walk around the class. Talk with your classmates. Ask their opinions about cities in your country.

CULTURE TIP

Try to find out your partner's opinion. This "balances" the conversation.
"How about you?"
"What do you think?"

BASIC CONVERSATION

Excuse me. Do you like ....?
    Yes, I do.
Why do you like it?
    Well, it's...
Which city do you like better:
_____ or _____?

BONUS

Try to use some of these expressions.

STARTING AND STOPPING
• Excuse me. I'd like to ask your opinion.
• Thanks. It's been fun talking to you.

ASKING
• Which city do you think is more...., A or B?
• Don't you think that (it's dangerous)?

ANSWERING
• I don't like it because when I was there...
• I've heard it's a nice place.

6 VOCABULARY BUILDING

Work with a partner. Look at each phrase. Can you think of a city?
Don't say the same city twice!

- has a lot of taxi cabs
- has crowded subways
- has musicians playing on the street
- has a lot of homeless people
- has noisy traffic
- has a lot of skyscrapers
- has too much pollution

- has a lot of traffic problems
- has beautiful buildings
- has a lot of modern architecture
- has a river running through it
- has a lot of historical sites
- has religious significance
- has too many tourists

7 SMALL TALK: WHAT I LIKE ABOUT THIS CITY

Recently, a group of people in Dallas, Texas, were asked what they think about their hometown. Here are some of their ideas:

"Must have" items
- silver rings
- cutoff shorts from CK™ jeans
- Jansport™ backpacks

DALLAS

Favorite sports team:
The Dallas Cowboys

Worst stereotype:
"Everybody thinks we speak with a southern accent, but we don't."

Best feature of the city:
Good weather all year round

Most popular entertainment:
Six Flags Over Texas (amusement park). Best ride is the Texas Giant roller-coaster

Most popular shopping spot:
The Galleria Shopping Center—It has an ice-skating rink inside. The best shop—"Wild at Heart," noted for its large T-shirt collection

Talk about these questions with your classmates.

> *What are some "must have" items among your friends?*

> *Do people in your city have a special accent?*

> *What is the worst stereotype about people in your city?*

8 COMMUNICATION TASK — *City Portrait*

Work with a partner. Create a collage (draw sketches or images) that represents your city.

collage for _____
city

Best feature

Favorite sports team

Worst stereotype

Your idea:

"Must have" items

Most popular shopping spot

Most popular amusement

COMMUNICATION
GOAL

Whose collage is the most interesting?

Now join another pair. Ask questions about their collage.

9 GRAMMAR CHECK

Write a sentence that has a similar meaning.

Example: Chicago is hotter than Osaka in the summer.
       Osaka is cooler than Chicago in the summer.

1. Mexico City is warmer than Ontario.

2. Rome has fewer people than New Delhi.

3. Prices in Prague are lower than in Seoul.

4. There is more traffic in Bangkok than in Melbourne.

5. Victoria isn't as populated as Dallas.

6. Athens isn't as noisy as Jakarta.

7. Hong Kong has more stores than Los Angeles.

8. Paris isn't as cold as Dublin.

9. There are fewer cities in New Zealand than in Russia.

10. There are more people in Tokyo than in Singapore.

16 Jobs

GRAMMAR TARGETS

Jobs	What kind of work	do you do?	I'm	an actor.
	What			a teacher.

Routines	What do you **have to**	**do** in your job?		
		do at work?		
		do there?		
	Most of the time	I	**answer** the phone.	
	Sometimes		**visit** clients.	
	I	**often**	travel to other countries	
		hardly ever	talk to patients.	

Opinions	Do you	like	**it**?	Yes,	I	**love** my job.
		enjoy		No,	I	**don't like** working there.

WARM UP *Name three jobs you would love to have.*

1 CONVERSATION

Look at the picture. *Where are they? What is happening?*

Fill in the missing words. Then listen and check your answers.

Andy: What do you do?

Laura: _____? I work for Spielberg
I   Me
Studios.

Andy: Really? What do you do _____?
them   there

Laura: I'm a film _____.
editing   editor

Andy: A film editor? Wow, _____
this   that
sounds interesting. Do you enjoy it?

Laura: Well, it's not _____
that   such
interesting. _____ time, I
Most of   Most of the
just work in a small editing room.

Andy: _____ work with
Do you ever   Have you ever
the film directors?

Laura: Sometimes, but not
_____ often.
very   really

Now practice the conversation.

2 LISTENING 📟

Listen and write the correct information. What is their job? What is their opinion about it?

1. Niles:
   Job: ....

   Opinion: ....

2. Rachel:
   Job: ....

   Opinion: ....

3 PRONUNCIATION TIP 📟

HOW TO

Reduce "of"

If you reduce short grammar words like "of", you'll sound more natural.

Reduce "of" before a consonant	→	ə
Connect /ə/ to the word before it.	→	most‿ə
Speak smoothly.	→	most‿ə the time

Listen. Mark the stressed syllables.

1. What kind of work do you do?
2. Most of the time, I just work in a small editing room.
3. What sort of company do you work for?
4. Almost all of the time, I stay in the office.
5. Some of the time, I visit clients.
6. A lot of the time, I just answer the phone.

Listen again and repeat. Reduce "of" to /ə/ and connect. Speak smoothly.

4 PRACTICE

Work with a partner. Look at each job.
Say one good point and one bad point about each job.

EXAMPLE

What's a good point of being
a professional baseball player?
   You can become famous.
What's a bad point?
   You have to travel a lot.

a professional baseball player
a teacher
a cowboy
a bartender
a musician
a cook
a window cleaner
a carpenter

5 EXCHANGE

Choose one of the jobs in Section 4 (Practice), or think of a new job. Walk around the classroom. Meet other people and ask about their "jobs".

BASIC CONVERSATION

What do you do?
I'm a...
That sounds interesting. Do you enjoy it?

BONUS

Try to use some of these expressions.

ASKING
• What sort of work do you do?
• What company are you at?

ANSWERING
• I'm in business. I sell stocks.
• I work at home. I'm a homemaker.

WHEN YOU DON'T WORK
• I'm a student.
• I'm between jobs right now.

6 VOCABULARY BUILDING

Match the job in the left column with a function on the right.

actor	creates works of art
musician	organizes and runs a household
artist	watches over people who are swimming at a beach or pool
teacher	interviews guests in front of a studio or television audience
referee	works in television dramas, in movies, or in plays
talk show host	greets visitors at a company or hotel
homemaker	helps students gain knowledge and skills
lifeguard	performs in recording sessions or in front of audiences
film editor	tries to cure patients' illnesses
receptionist	keeps order during a game or match
doctor	works with a movie after it has been shot

7 SMALL TALK: WORKAHOLICS

Many people are "workaholics." They love to work, they need to work to be happy, and they are always thinking about their work. And they don't know what to do unless they're working.

Jay Leno is a comedian and television talk show host. He basically works all the time. Leno sleeps only four hours a night and the rest of the time he's working: preparing comedy skits for his show, preparing acts for his comedy performances at comedy clubs, reviewing tapes of his shows, or rehearsing.

Does Leno ever take a vacation? "Vacation? I don't like to take vacations," Leno says. "If I take a vacation, I lose my edge. I can't stay sharp. And being sharp is what this business is all about."

Talk about these questions with your classmates.

Are you a workaholic?

Do you know any "workaholics"?

8 COMMUNICATION TASK  *The Perfect Job*

What is your dream job?
Work with a partner. Ask each other the following questions.

1. Where would you like to work?

2. Who would you like to work with?

with many people?   with a few people?   alone?

3. How hard would you want to work?

4. What hours would you like to work?

5. How much pay would you like per year?

6. (other question)

7. (other question)

8. (other question)

suggestion:

COMMUNICATION

GOAL

What jobs did your partners suggest for you?

Now suggest a job for your partner.
Does your partner agree with your suggestion?   Now interview a new partner.

9 GRAMMAR CHECK

Fill in the blanks in each sentence.

1. What .... of work do you do?
2. Do you .... your work?
3. What sort .... company do you work ....?
4. Most .... time I work at a computer.
5. What is .... good point of being a doctor?
6. Your work .... interesting. Do you enjoy it?
7. I work .... home. I'm .... homemaker.
8. What do you .... to do in your job?
9. I teach advanced English ....
10. It's .... difficult job, but I like ....

Now make 10 conversations, using these sentences.

GRAMMAR TARGETS

Questions about the past	Are you still	working at living in	NEC? Tokyo?	Yes, I **am**. No, I'**m not**.		
	Do you remember	your first	boyfriend/girlfriend? day at school?	Yes, I No,	**do**. **don't**.	
	What kind of	teacher **was** car	she? it?	She It	**was**	very strict. a Ford Mustang.
Statements about the past	I liv**ed**	in the States with my parents at school	when I **was** in elementary school. a long time ago. for several years.			
	I **used to**	**talk** on the phone **swim**	every day. every summer.			

WARM UP *Do you remember your favorite game when you were a child? Do you remember your best friend?*

1 CONVERSATION

Look at the picture. *Where are they? What is happening?*

Fill in the missing words. Then listen and check your answers.

Mary: Matt? Matt Jergen?

Matt: Hey, it's good to see you, Mary. How long _____ it been?

                       is   has

Mary: Wow. It's been _____ a

                       so   such
long time. What? Five or six years?

Matt: Right. It was at your wedding. _____ Brian?

                 How's   Who's

Mary: Actually, we split _____ about a year ago.

             out   up

Matt: Oh, I'm sorry _____ hear that.

             to   for

Mary: Yeah. Thanks.

Now practice the conversation.

2 LISTENING 📻

Listen and check the true statements.

1. Diane and Michael:
- ❏ a. Diane and Michael went to school together.
- ❏ b. Diane lives in Boston.
- ❏ c. Michael lives in New York.
- ❏ d. They are happy to see each other.

2. Peter and Misa:
- ❏ a. Peter and Misa graduated five years ago.
- ❏ b. Peter is going to law school.
- ❏ c. Peter is an actor.
- ❏ d. Misa is living in the U.S.

3 PRONUNCIATION TIP 📻

HOW TO

Reduce the Verbs "be" and "have"

Most forms of "be" and "have" have weak stress. If you reduce them, you'll sound more natural.

Full Stressed Form	Reduced Unstressed Form	
am	/əm/	I'm sorry to **hear** that.
are	/ər/	Y*ər* Mary **Hillman**!
is	/s/	It's good to **see** you.
is	/z/	How'*z* **Brian**?
has	/əz/	How long*əz* it **been**?
has	/s/	It's b*ɪn* a long **time**.
been	/bɪn/ or /bən/	
was	/wəz/	It w*əz* at your **wedding**.
were	/wər/	We w*ər* **married** about five **years**.

Listen. Repeat the weak forms.
Then repeat the whole sentence. Say everything in one breath.

1. /əm/
I'm sorry to **hear** that.

2. /ər/
You're Mary **Hill**man!

3. /s/
It's good to **see** you!

4. /z/
How's **Brian**?

5. /əz/
How long has it **been**?

6. /bən/
It's been a long **time**.

7. /wəz/
It was at your **wedding**.

8. /wər/
We were **married** about five **years**.

4 PRACTICE

Work with a partner. Ask your partner about 5 memories.

EXAMPLE	your childhood friends	the foods you used to eat
Do you remember _____? *Yes. It was. . . .*	your childhood toys	some sports you played
your first report card at school	a time when you got hurt	some happy events
your first love	your bedroom as a child	the places you have lived
your first teacher	your boyfriends or girlfriends	your favorite childhood snack
your favorite place to play	your first report card at school	your elementary school teachers

5 EXCHANGE

Walk around the class. Talk to your classmates. Ask them about memories they have.

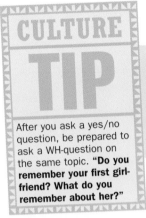

CULTURE TIP

After you ask a yes/no question, be prepared to ask a WH-question on the same topic. **"Do you remember your first girlfriend? What do you remember about her?"**

BASIC CONVERSATION

Do you remember your first teacher?
Yes, her name was...
What kind of teacher was she?
She was...

BONUS

Try to use some of these expressions.

ASKING
• Do you have any memories of...?
• Do you remember anything about...?

ANSWERING
• I don't remember much. I only remember...
• Gosh, it was a long time ago. I think...

TALKING ABOUT SOMETHING THAT MAY BE PERSONAL
• If it's not too personal, what happened to your father?
• Sorry, I'd rather not talk about it.

6 VOCABULARY BUILDING

Put these words in "time order".

When I was ...

• a baby
• a college student
• a grad student
• a grade school pupil
• a high school student
• a little kid
• a middle school pupil
• a toddler
• a young adult
• in middle age
• in my 20s
• in my early 30s

.... **birth**
                                             ....
....
                                             ....
....
                                             ....
....
                                             ....
....
                                             ....
                                             ....

7 SMALL TALK: MEMORIES

Most people can always recall little songs and rhymes they learned in childhood. Here are some common American children's rhymes and songs. Have you heard of these?

The Star

Twinkle, twinkle, little star,
how I wonder what you are!
Up above the world so high,
like a diamond in the sky

The Church

This is the church.

This is the steeple.

Open the doors.

And see all the people!

Talk about these questions with your classmates.

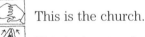

Do you remember any childhood songs?

Do you remember any childhood "hand rhymes"?

What were your favorite childhood games?

8 COMMUNICATION TASK — Memory Madness

Play this game in teams of three.

STEPS

1. Form teams. Your teacher will pick a topic.
2. Go around the class. Each team must say one item for each topic. Each answer = one point. Pass = no points.

EXAMPLE

Pop Stars
    Eric Clapton...
    Madonna...
    Elvis Presley...

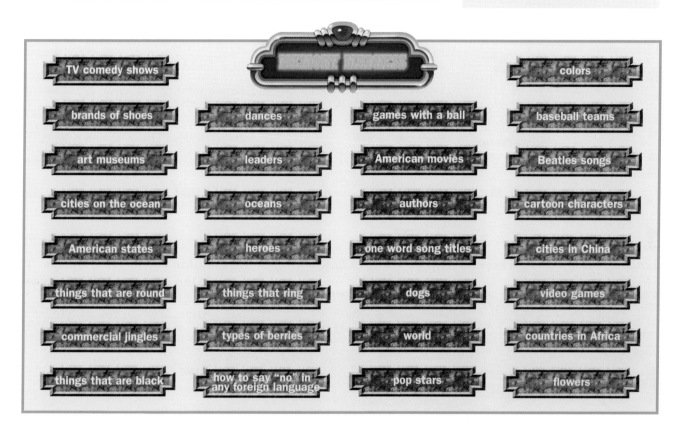

- TV comedy shows
- brands of shoes
- art museums
- cities on the ocean
- American states
- things that are round
- commercial jingles
- things that are black
- dances
- leaders
- oceans
- heroes
- things that ring
- types of berries
- how to say "no" in any foreign language
- games with a ball
- American movies
- authors
- one word song titles
- dogs
- world
- pop stars
- colors
- baseball teams
- Beatles songs
- cartoon characters
- cities in China
- video games
- countries in Africa
- flowers

9 GRAMMAR CHECK

Work with a partner. Partner A, read sentences 1-5 out loud; Partner B, write the sentences on a sheet of paper. (Don't look at the book!)
Partner B, read sentences 6-10; Partner A, write the sentences on a sheet of paper.

1. I remember you—you're Michael Clark.

2. It's good to see you. It's been a long time.

3. Yes, it's been at least five years.

4. That's right. The last time I saw you was at Mary's wedding.

5. How have you been?

6. I've been fine. How about you?

7. Just great.

8. Do you remember when we were in high school together?

9. Of course, I remember that time very well.

10. We had a lot of good times together.

Check your sentences by looking in the book.

18 Trends

GRAMMAR TARGETS

Desires				
	I **wish**	you he they	**would**	**go** salsa dancing with me. **try** jogging. **eat** healthier meals.
	I **wish**	she Tony	**wouldn't**	**watch** so much TV. **go out** in this weather.
Opinions—Agreeing	**I think** smoking is dangerous. **I'm opposed to** smoking.		I **do**, too. /So **do** I. I **am**, too./So **am** I.	I don't (think so). I'm not.
	I don't think smoking is dangerous. **I'm not opposed to** smoking.		I **don't either**./Neither **do** I. **I'm not, either**./Neither **am** I.	I do. I am.
Opinions—Disagreeing	Smoking **is** dangerous. Smoking **isn't** so dangerous.		I think so, **too**. I don't think so, **either**.	I **don't** think **so**. I think **it is**.

WARM UP *What are some current trends in fashion, education and food?*

1 CONVERSATION

Look at the picture. *Where are they? What is happening?*

Fill in the missing words. Then listen and check your answers.

Alice: Why do you watch _____ (such / so) violent TV programs?

Tom: Oh, Mom. This show _____ (isn't / doesn't) violent.

Alice: Yes, it is. I _____ (hope / wish) you _____ (don't / wouldn't) watch that kind of stuff.

Tom: Oh, come on. It's not _____ (as / that) bad.

Alice: Sorry. You'll _____ (must / have to) turn it off.

Tom: Aw, Mom.

Now practice the conversation

2 LISTENING 📼

Listen and write the correct information. What are they talking about? What is their opinion?

1. Sandy and Carla:
   Talking about: _____
   Sandy's opinion: _____

2. Larry and Josh:
   Talking about: _____
   Larry's opinion: _____

3 PRONUNCIATION TIP 📼

Stretch the important words.

"Why do you watch TV programs like that?
They're **t-o-o v-i-o-l-e-n-t!**"

Listen. Mark the stressed syllables.

1. A: What do you think of bodybuilding?
   B: I think it's silly.

2. A: I always eat at fast-food restaurants.
   B: That's crazy!

3. A: I think an American diet is bad for you.
   B: It's not that bad.

4. A: What do you think of using
      cellular phones?
   B: It's too expensive!

Listen again and repeat. Really s-t-r-e-t-c-h the words that show your opinion.

4 PRACTICE

Work with a partner. Point to a topic. Ask a question. Your partner will give an opinion.

EXAMPLE

What do you think about _____?
   I think it's _____.

eating at fast food restaurants

using cellular phones

body-building

in-line skating

playing the lottery

watching violent movies

Now think of one more topic. Ask your partner about it.

5 EXCHANGE

Stand up. Walk around the class.
Talk to your classmates.
Ask their opinions about three different topics.

CULTURE TIP

Show agreement wherever you can.
"Yes, I know what you mean." "Hmm. Maybe you're right." "I agree with you about that..."

BASIC CONVERSATION

Excuse me. Can I ask you about something?
Sure. What is it?
What do you think of...?
I think they're...

BONUS

Try to use some of these expressions.

ASKING
- I think _____. What do you think?
- Do you have an opinion about _____?

ANSWERING
- I don't have a strong opinion, but...
- I think it depends on...

SHOWING AGREEMENT/DISAGREEMENT
- Oh, that's a good point.
- Yes, I see what you mean.
- Really? I had a different experience.

6 VOCABULARY BUILDING

Here are some trends and ideas. Match each trend with your own opinion about it.

I think that

eating health food
riding skateboards
home exercise equipment
using Rollerblades
listening to a Walkman
using a cell phone
using a laptop computer
•
•

is

a waste of money
dangerous
fun
necessary
stupid
crazy
unnecessary
a good idea
a great idea
a brilliant idea

Think of two more trends. Now compare your sentences with a partner.

7 SMALL TALK: ENGLISH FOR COMMUNICATION

English is taught in different ways around the world. In many places, teachers still use the "grammar translation method." The key points of this method are:

- Use model sentences.
- Analyze the grammar and explain grammar rules.
- The students work in class translating into and from English.
- The teacher corrects all grammar mistakes.
- Emphasize memorizing vocabulary and translations.

In other places, teachers use the "communicative language method." The key points of this method are:

- Use model conversations.
- Emphasize speaking and listening.
- Focus on meaning; don't analyze the grammar.
- The students work in class, speaking in pairs or groups.
- Emphasize communication of ideas.

Talk about these questions with your classmates.

What kind of teaching method is used to teach English in your country?

What do you think is the best way to learn "English for communication"?

8 COMMUNICATION TASK

Choose one of the topics below. Answer the questions. Then write one more question.

ENGLISH TRENDS

Should students use English only during English class?

Should all children learn some English?

your question:

EDUCATION TRENDS

What are the best ways to teach?

Should teachers be allowed to use corporal (physical) punishment?

your question:

MODERN LIFESTYLES

What is the best part about people's lifestyles today?

How will our lifestyles change in the future?

your question:

MODERN TECHNOLOGY

Do you think computers are good for us?

What machine do you hope will be invented soon?

your question:

MODERN BEAUTY

Do you think modern beauty products are good?

What beauty products do you use?

your question:

COMMUNICATION

GOAL

Whose opinions surprised you?

•

Now work in a group of 4. Ask your questions to the group.

9 GRAMMAR CHECK

Put the following conversations into order.

_1_   I wish you wouldn't wear such short skirts.

_____ Yes, I do. I think that this skirt looks good on me.

_____ Oh, Mom, I'm 15 years old. I think I should be able to decide what to wear.

_____ Well, I think it looks terrible. Do you think that wearing short skirts is attractive?

_____ What's your opinion about people who talk on the phone while they are driving?

_____ I think they're being very dangerous. How about you?

_____ Yeah, I wish the government would pass a law making it illegal.

_____ Me, too. I think that people shouldn't drive and talk on the phone.

Now cover the conversations. Can you remember them?
Practice the conversations with a partner.

ACTIVITY 1 SPEAKING CIRCLES

GRAMMAR TARGETS

Simple Present Perfect	Would you like a cup of coffee?	No, thank you. I**'ve** already **had** one. Thank you. I **haven't had** one yet.
With *ever*, to ask about experience	**Have** you ever **been** to London?	Yes, I have. I**'ve been** there several times. No, I haven't. I**'ve never been** there.
With *for* and *since*, to talk about duration	How long **have** you **lived** here?	I **have lived** here for two years.
	How long **have** you **been** on vacation?	I **have been** on vacation since Monday.
Present Perfect to emphasize continuity	How long **have** you **been** working here?	I**'ve been** working here since 1981.

❶ Sit in two rows. Face each other.
❷ Start with TOPIC 1.
❸ Talk to your partner for 1 minute.
❹ Then change partners.
❺ Talk for 1 minute about the same topic.
❻ Continue for 3 or 4 partners.
❼ Start again on TOPIC 2 with a new partner.

CONVERSATION TIP

Encourage your partner to speak. Keep asking questions.

TOPIC 1

VACATIONS

Sample questions:
Do you know a good place to go to practice my English?
Where would you go if you could travel to any country?

TOPIC 2

CITIES

Sample questions:
What is your favorite city in the world?
Do you like visiting big cities?

TOPIC 3

JOBS

Sample questions:
What do you do?
Do you have a part-time or full-time job?
Do you enjoy your job?
What do you have to do at work?

TOPIC 4

MEMORIES

Sample questions:
Do you remember your first heartbreak?
If you could go back to being a child, would you?

TOPIC 5

TRENDS

Sample questions:
Do you think it's important to be fashionable?
What do you think of the current fashions?
Do you think that smoking in public is OK?
What's your opinion about school uniforms?

ACTIVITY 2 ROLE PLAY

**Work with a partner. Choose a situation. Make up a dialogue.
Practice your dialogue. Then say your dialogue in front of the class.**

EXAMPLE

Two friends are talking about their vacations.

Wing: I spent two weeks in Kenya last summer.
Have you ever been there?
Marsha: *No, but I went to Uganda once
for a few weeks.*
Wing: I've never been there. Did you enjoy it?
Marsha: *Yes, a lot. It's a beautiful country.
I'd love to go back some day.*

CULTURE TIP

Use gestures to help
people understand you.

SITUATION 1

Two people trying to decide where to go on vacation

Possible Expressions:

Where do you want to go?

Do you want to go to Bali?

I went there three years ago.

We haven't been to Europe since 1992.

SITUATION 2

A person discussing moving to another city with a friend

Possible Expressions:

What do you think of Kyoto?

Which do you like better: Tokyo or Kyoto?

Kyoto is less crowded than Tokyo.

You have been living here for 10 years.
Why move?

SITUATION 3

A person at a job interview

Possible Expressions:

How long did you work at Sybase?

What do I have to do here?

I worked for Sybase for one year.

We have been in business since 1933.

SITUATION 4

Two parents discussing their teenage kids

Possible Expressions:

What's your opinion about kids driving at 16?

Do you think kids should be able to pierce
their bodies?

I wish my son wouldn't smoke cigarettes.

I think my kids need to go to summer school
this year.

SITUATION 5

Two people at a high school reunion

Possible Expressions:

Are you still living here in town?

Do you remember Stan? What ever
happened to him?

We used to talk on the phone for hours
every night.

I moved to New York four years ago.

UNIT 1 LISTENING

1. A: Hi. Are you in Ms. Hill's English class?
   B: Yes.
   A: I'm in that class, too. I usually sit two rows behind you.
   B: Oh, hi. What do you think of the class?
   A: I love it. She's a great teacher. I learn something new every day.
   B: Yeah, I'm enjoying it, too.

2. A: Hello. How are you?
   B: Fine, thank you.
   A: We haven't met yet. I'm Brian from the marketing department.
   B: Hi, Brian. I'm Catherine.
   A: You're the new person in the art department, right?
   B: Yeah, that's me.
   A: How do you like working here?
   B: It's fun. I really like the people I work with.
   A: Yeah, this is a great company to work for.

UNIT 2 LISTENING

1. A: Stephanie, I've got to go. Can I call you later?
   B: Sure.
   A: What's your phone number?
   B: It's 555-2875.
   A: The area code is 510?
   B: No, it's 415.
   A: When is the best time to call?
   B: Oh, any time after 7 is fine.

2. A: Say, Tom, why don't I come by your office sometime?
   B: Good idea. My company is called Independent Business Products.
   A: What's the address?
   B: It's 1542 Gough Street. It's in downtown Chicago.
   A: How do you spell Gough?
   B: It's G-O-U-G-H. My office is on the fifth floor. We're in Suite 520.
   A: Great. What's a good time to stop by?
   B: I'm there from about 10 until 5 or so every weekday.

UNIT 3 LISTENING

1. A: Hi, Beth. Long time, no see.
   B: Hi, Marcia.
   A: Is your hair different?
   B: Yeah, I got it done last week. What do you think?
   A: It's interesting. I've never seen hair dyed that color before.
   B: Thanks, I guess.
   A: No, I mean that your hair looks great. It's just a bit strange, that's all.

2. A: That sweater looks great on you, Karen. It's really your color.
   B: Thanks. It's new.
   A: Where did you get it?
   B: My boyfriend got it for me.
   A: Looks comfortable.
   B: Yeah, it is.
   A: You're lucky to have such a nice boyfriend. Mine never buys me anything.

UNIT 4 LISTENING

1. A: What did you do this weekend?
   B: Not much. I drove to Monterey on Saturday.
   A: To do what?
   B: Oh, I just wanted to take a walk on the beach.
   A: Sounds relaxing.
   B: Yeah, it was. It was nice.

2. A: Did you do anything this weekend?
   B: Yeah, I went to the Wallflowers concert on Friday. It was great.
   A: Oh, really. Was it at the Fillmore Theater?
   B: Yep.
   A: Crowded?
   B: Yeah, it was really crowded, but we had good seats.
   A: Who did you go with?
   B: Jeremy. We had a great time.

UNIT 5 LISTENING

1. A: Did your parents give you anything for your birthday?
   B: Yeah, you won't believe this. Look — they gave me my own cell phone.
   A: Gosh, a pink cell phone.
   B: Yeah, and it's so small it fits in my pocket.
   A: Oh, wow. The buttons are shiny. They light up.
   B: Right. You can use it even in the dark.
   A: That's an expensive gift!
   B: I know.

2. A: What is this?
   B: It's a clock.
   A: It looks like an old plastic record.
   B: Yeah, it is an old record, but it has a clock in the middle of it.
   A Interesting.
   B: Yeah, my son made it. He likes making strange art objects like this.
   A: Hmm.
   B: Yeah, he calls it a record-clock.

UNIT 6 LISTENING

1. A: I'm bored. Do you want to do something?
   B: I don't know. Where would you like to go?
   A: Have you eaten? We could go out for dinner.
   B: Food sounds good. What kind do you want?
   A: I sort of feel like pizza, but I know you don't like it that much.
   B: Well, let's go to an Italian restaurant where you can get pizza and I can get pasta.
   A: Great. I'll get my coat.

2. A: What do you want to do on Sunday?
   B: Sunday? Are you kidding? The big game is on TV. I'm spending Sunday right here.
   A: That's boring. All you do is watch sports. Let's do something special. How about a drive to Carmel?
   B: I don't know. OK, I'll go, but I get to listen to the game in the car.
   A: All right. It's a deal.

Pronunciation
1. What do you want to do tonight?
2. Do you want to go to a movie?
3. She wants to go to a movie.
4. She wants to go to the 9:15 show.
5. Do you want to go for a drive?
6. He wants to stay home.
7. Do you want to see a play tomorrow?
8. He doesn't want to do anything.

UNIT 7 LISTENING

1. A: Pavel, you were born in Russia, weren't you?
   B: Actually, I am Ukrainian. I was born in Kiev.
   A: You are awfully far from your country. Do you miss home?
   B: Yes, very much.
   A: If you don't mind me asking, what do you miss the most?
   B: Of course, I miss my family. My parents are still living in Kiev.

2. A: You know, Maria, we've been friends for almost a year, and I don't know where you were born.
   B: I was born in Mexico.
   A: Really? I didn't know you were Mexican. You know, you never talk about Mexico.
   B: Well, I lived there a long time ago. I was born in Mexico, but I've lived here over 20 years.
   A: Do you still get homesick?
   B: Not very much, but sometimes I miss speaking Spanish.

UNIT 8 LISTENING

1. A: Your apartment is nice. Didn't you just move in?
   B: Yeah, I just moved in two days ago.
   A: Two days ago! You're kidding! It's so neat. It looks like you've been here forever.
   B: Well, I didn't have very much stuff to unpack, and I hate having a messy apartment.
   A: Amazing.

2. A: I haven't seen you lately.
   B: I've been so busy with the move.
   A: Oh, that's right. You just bought a new house. Do you like it?
   B: Oh yes! It's a lot bigger than our old house.
   A: Really?
   B: Yeah, our old house had only two bedrooms. The new one has three bedrooms and a study. The kids are much happier now that they don't have to share a bedroom.
   A: Right, I can imagine.

UNIT 9 LISTENING

1. A: You know, Tim, I think I have to find a better paying job. I don't earn enough at my job now.
   B: What are you talking about. Debra? You have a great job. Your salary is almost double mine.
   A: Yeah, but I owe so much money to people that I can't save any.
   B: Really? Who do you owe money to?
   A: I still have a student loan to pay off — that's $400 a month — and I owe my credit card company over $3,000.
   B: Wow, you need to learn how to budget your money.

2. A: You're going to travel to Europe next summer?
   B: Yep.
   A: How are you going to afford that, Jack?
   B: Saving. I'm saving about $250 of my salary each month.
   B: How much do you need?
   A: About $2,000. I'm almost there.
   B: Well, good for you. I couldn't do that.
   A: It's easy. I'm really good at saving money when it's for something fun.

UNIT 10 LISTENING

1. A: Mary, I think I'm in love. Who is that man wearing those sexy sunglasses?
   B: Do you mean Ted?
   A: No, I know Ted. I mean the guy talking to him.
   B: The one in the leather jacket?
   A: Yeah, who is that?
   B: That's Tony. You wouldn't like him. Believe me. He looks cool, but he isn't very nice.
   A: Oh, that's too bad. I'm kind of attracted to him.

2. A: I just met Tanya. She sure is good-looking.
   B: Boy, is she! Have you ever seen such beautiful, long hair?
   A: I know. And she has a great personality, too. Does she have a boyfriend?
   B: Worse. She has a husband.
   A: It figures.

UNIT 11 LISTENING

1. A: Pardon me, sir?
   B: Yes.
   A: I'm a little lost. Do you happen to know where the Tower Building is?
   B: Oh, sure. That's on Fifth Avenue. The corner of Fifth and Rose.
   A: I'm afraid I don't know where that is.
   B: All you need to do is walk down this street until you get to Fifth Avenue. Turn left on Fifth and you will see the building on your right.
   A: Thanks a lot.

2. A: Can you come and pick me up?
   B: I guess so. Where are you?
   A: I'm at Matt's house. Do you know where that is?
   B: No.
   A: It's on Caldwell Street. 4531 Caldwell Street. Just take Green Street one block past Main Street, and then turn right.
   B: Is it on the right side or the left side?
   A: It'll be on your left side. It's a big green house. You can't miss it.

UNIT 12 LISTENING

1. A: Do you know how often the train comes?
   B: There should be a train every seven minutes, but I've been waiting for 15 minutes.
   A: Oh, no. Is that the correct time, 7:45?
   B: Yes, that's right.
   A: Oh, no. That train better get here soon or I'm going to be in trouble.
   B: Why?
   A: I have to be to work at 8:30. My boss said if I was late again, he would fire me.

2. A: Do you want to play another game?
   B: Sure — hey wait a minute. What time is it?
   A: It's 10 after 10.
   B: No way! I got to go.
   A: Come on. Just one more game.
   B: No, I can't. I really can't. I told Sue I would be home at 10:00 this time. She's going to kill me.

UNIT 13 LISTENING

1. A: Darn it!
   B: What's wrong?
   A: I have to fax this order to the head office and this fax machine won't work.
   B: Maybe I can help.
   A: Do you know how to work this?
   B: Yeah, I think so. Did you dial the phone number?
   A: Yes. I'm not stupid, you know.
   B: OK, OK. Calm down. Did you press the send button?
   A: Ugh. . . no, I guess I forgot to do that.

2. A: Brett, could you come here for a minute, please?
   B: Yes, what is it, Ms. Miller?
   A: I'm trying to make some coffee, but this coffee maker is broken. We need to buy a new one.
   B: Just a second. Can I have a look? I think this machine is all right. Oh, you just have to pour in some water before you turn it on.
   A: Of course! How did I forget the water?
   B: Well, you have been very busy lately, ma'am.

UNIT 14 LISTENING

1. A: So, Bob, you have two weeks off. Where are you going on your vacation?
   B: Actually, I'm going to Paris.
   A: Paris? I didn't know that. What are you going to do in Paris?
   B: Tons of stuff, but mostly I want to visit the art museums. I've always wanted to see the Mona Lisa.
   A: That's at the Louvre, right?
   B: Yes, I'm going to spend one whole day there, if I can.

2. A: I'm going home for Christmas vacation. Where are you going?
   B: I'm going to New York City.
   A: Oh, I love New York. The plays, the shopping, the restaurants. What are you planning on doing there?
   B: You know, since I've never been there, I want to go sightseeing.
   A: Well, make sure you see the Statue of Liberty. It's New York's number one tourist spot.
   B: Oh, no question. I'm going to be sure to see that.

UNIT 15 LISTENING

1. A: Nina, now that you're settled in, I've been meaning to ask you: What do you think of living in Rio de Janeiro?
   B: I love it! The only problem is that it's very crowded.
   A: Yes, there are a lot of people here.
   B: But the people are so friendly. It's a very lively city. You can go out and do something 24 hours a day.
   A: I'm glad you like it.
   B: Like it? I love it.

2. A: Well, dear, how is Florence? Is it what you expected?
   B: Oh, Dad, it's wonderful. There is so much history here. It's so interesting. Yesterday I went to Michelangelo's house.
   A: I'm glad you're enjoying yourself, but remember you have to come home next week.
   B: Oh, I wish I could stay here forever. It's so beautiful. I would never get bored here.

UNIT 16 LISTENING

1. A: How do you do? My name's Niles.
   B: Hello, Niles. I'm Katrina. Is this your first conference?
   A: Yes, I'm a new stockbroker over at Smith Brothers.
   B: Really? I'm a broker at Charles Swab. Do you like it?
   A: It's OK. It's a very stressful job.
   B: I know just what you mean. I usually work about 70 hours a week.
   A: Me, too.

2. A: Martha told me that you were a high school teacher.
   B: Yeah, I teach math at Ben Franklin High.
   A: Really? When I was younger I used to teach math to junior high school students.
   B: Oh, did you enjoy it?
   A: I loved it. I would still be doing it if I hadn't retired.
   B: I like it, too. Being around the students keeps me young.

UNIT 17 LISTENING

1. A: Excuse me. You look familiar. Do I know you?
   B: I don't think so. Wait! Diane? Diane Green?
   A: Yeah. Oh, I can't believe it. Michael Slattery! I haven't seen you since high school. How are you?
   B: Great. Are you still living in Boston?
   A: No, I moved years ago. I live here in New York. What about you?
   B: I'm just here on business.

2. A: Gosh, Peter, it's been a long time.
   B: It sure has. Can you believe we graduated five years ago? What have you been doing since graduation, Misa?
   A: Oh, I moved to Thailand. I teach English in Bangkok. I'm just back for a visit. What about you?
   B: Remember how I was going to go to law school? Well, I dropped out and decided to be an actor instead.
   A: No kidding? Your parents must have been upset about that.
   B: Well, they weren't too thrilled.

UNIT 18 LISTENING

1. A: Sandy, it's Carla. I'm just about to go jogging. Do you want to go?
   B: No, not today. It's snowing! Why do you go jogging so much?
   A: I'm training for the marathon.
   B: Really? You're going to run in the New York marathon?
   A: Yeah, just four more months.
   B: Carla, come on. Give it up. That's crazy. It'll kill you.

2. A: Larry, how was your blind date?
   B: It was OK... Actually, it was sort of boring.
   A: Why? Wasn't she an interesting person?
   B: I don't know. She was really shy. She didn't say more than 10 words during dinner.
   A: Are you going to ask her out again?
   B: I don't think so. And I'm not going to try blind dates any more. It's just...embarrassing.

Strategies in Speaking uses 500 key expressions

The number after the expression shows the unit in which the expression first appears. The number 1-18 refer to the main units; F1-4, F5-9, F10-13, F14-18 refer to the fluency units.

"FORMULA" EXPRESSIONS

All right. 6
Amazing. 8
Are you kidding? 6
Aw,(Mom). 18
Believe me. 10
Boy, is she (attractive)! 10
Bye. 12
Can you believe it? 17
Come on. It'll be fun. 6
Darn it! 13
Darn! 4
Do I know you? 17
Don't feel bad. 13
Don't worry. 15
Excuse me. 11
Give it up. 18
Go ahead. 12
Good for you. 9
Gosh, it was a long time ago. 17
Gosh. 5
Great (shoes)! 3
Hey, that's an attractive (jacket). 3
Hi, my name's... F1-4
Hm... 10
How did I forget (that)? 13
I can't believe it. 17
I didn't know that. 14
I don't think so. 18
I don't think that's a good idea. 9
I forgot all about that! 4
I guess so. 11
I had a good time. 4
I know just what you mean. 16
I know what you mean. 1
I love it! 15
I love your tie. 3
I mean (the guy near the door). 10
I really like your (shoes). 3
I see what you mean. 18
I think it's a (great) idea. 18
I think it's (crazy). 18
I think it's a waste of money. 18
I think so, too. 10
I wish I could stay here forever. 15
I wish I had gone with you. 4
I'm sorry I missed it. 4
I'm a little lost. 11
I'm afraid I don't know ... 11
I'm almost there. 12
I'm bored. 6
I'm getting used to it. 15
I'm glad you like it. 3
I'm glad you're enjoying yourself. 15
I'm going to be sure to see that. 14
I'm not familiar with that. 7
I'm not stupid, you know. 13

I'm not sure, but I think it's... 11
I'm sorry to hear that. 7
I've got to go. 12
I've got to run. 2
I've heard it's a nice place. 15
It figures. 10
It looks like you've ... 8
It must be (my new hairstyle). 3
It was nice meeting you. 1
It was (pretty dull). 18
It'll kill you! 18
It's (enormous). 5
It's (super). 3
It's a deal. 6
It's a good thing you were here. 13
It's a little too crowded for me. 15
It's been a long time. 17
It's been such a long time. 17
It's good to see you. 17
It's great. 3
It's just embarrassing. 18
It's kind of (nice). 3
It's nice and big. F5-9
It's not my type. 3
It's not so big. 5
It's not so interesting for me. 1
It's OK, I guess. 3
It's OK. 3
It's pretty strange. 3
It's really beautiful. 3
It's so (neat). 8
It's very interesting. 3
It's worse than that. 10
Just a second. 13
Just one more (game). 12
Let me see. 13
Let's go. 6
Like it? I love it. 15
Maybe you should ask ... 11
Me, too. 10
My name is (Karen). 1
Neither.. 14
Nice talking to you. 2
Nice to meet you. 1
No kidding. 17
No problem. 11
No way! 12
No, I can't. 12
No, not today. 18
Nothing, really. 14
Of course! 13
Oh, (Mom)! 18
Oh, come on. It's not that bad. 18
Oh, gosh. 13
Oh, I just wanted to... 4
Oh, I love New York. 14
Oh, it's a little difficult, but... 15
Oh, it's beautiful. 5

Oh, it's nothing special. 3
Oh, no question. 14
Oh, no. 12
Oh, right. 14
Oh, sure. 11
Oh, thanks. 3
Oh, thanks for noticing. 3
Oh, that's a good point. 18
Oh, that's too bad. 10
Oh,(Dad), it's wonderful. 15
OK, OK. Calm down. 13
OK. See you later. 12
Ooh... 9
Ouch! 9
Pardon me, sir? 11
Really? 10
Right, I can imagine. 8
See you later. 2
She's going to kill me. 12
Sounds good. 6
Sounds perfect. 8
Sounds relaxing. 4
Stupid me! 13
Thank you. 3
Thanks a lot. 2
That looks great on you. F1-4
That sounds good. 6
That sounds like a great idea. 6
That'd be great. 2
That's (boring). 6
That's a (good) idea. 6
That's a nice (shirt). 3
Those are beautiful (earrings). 3
To do what? 4
Ugh, no, I guess I forgot... 13
Wait a minute. 12
We had a great time. 4
What a nice suit! 3
What about you? 17
What makes you say that? 10
What's wrong? 13
Which way? 11
Why do you say that? 10
Why do you think so? 15
Why do you think that? F10-13
Wow! 17
Yeah, I know what you mean. F1-4
Yeah, I think so. 12
Yes, that's right. 12
You can't miss it. 11
You look familiar. 17
You won't believe this... 5
You wouldn't like him. 10
You'll get used to it soon. 15
You're kidding! 8
You're right. 9

FUNCTIONAL EXPRESSIONS

Can I ask you for some advice? 9

Can I do something for you? 13

Can I have a look? 13

Can I have a raincheck? 6

Can I help you with anything? F10-13

Can I see it? 5

Can you come and pick me up? 11

Can you describe it for me? 5

Can you give me directions to (your house)? F10-13

Can you help me out? 13

Can you repeat them? 17

Can you say that again? 8

Could I ask you for some advice? 9

Could I borrow (your car)? 2

Could you come here for a minute, please? 13

Could you repeat that? 8

Do you happen to know where (the Tower Building) is? 11

Do you have an opinion on (that)? 18

Do you know (Macy's)? It's near that. 11

Do you know how often the train comes? 12

Do you know how to get there? F10-13

Do you know how to work this? 13

Do you know what machine I am talking about? 13

Do you know what time it is? 12

Do you know where that is? 11

Do you mean...? 8

Do you mind if I ask you some questions? 12

Do you want to (play another game)? 12

Do you want to do something? 6

Don't you think it's too expensive? F5-9

Excuse me, can I ask you a favor? 2

Excuse me. I didn't catch that. 2

Excuse me. I'd like to ask your opinion. 15

Have you been there long? 16

Have you eaten? 6

Have you ever met (Gill Brady)? 10

Hello, (Niles). I'm (Katrina). 16

How did you meet her? 3

How about a (drive to Carmel)? 6

How about you? 1

How are you? 17

How are you doing? 1

How do you do? 16

How do you know (Paul)? F1-4

How do you like it? 1

How do you use it? 13

How long does it take you to get to (school)? 12

How long has it been? 17

How many (windows) are there? 8

How much do you need? 9

How much does it cost? 9

How much is it? 9

I can't live without it. 13

I couldn't do that. 9

I don't have a strong opinion, but... 18

I didn't recognize you. 3

I don't need one. 13

I don't have it with me. 2

I don't want to see that. 6

I have other plans... 6

I haven't seen you lately. 8

I like it too. 1

I like it too, but... 1

I'll be out of town. 6

I like it. How about you? F1-4

I need to check my e-mail. 13

I really can't. 12

I think it depends on the situation. 18

I think it's fine. What do you think? 18

I wonder if I can ask you something? 2

I wonder if you'd like to (see a movie). 6

I'd like to talk more, but I've got to run. F10-13

I'm just about to (go jogging). Do you want to go? 18

I'm trying to find (Civic Station). 11

I'm trying to make some coffee, but... 13

If it's not too personal, what happened to (your father)? 17

Is that the correct time? 12

Is there a (post office) near here? 11

It'll be on (your right side). 11

It looks like a... 5

It's 10 after 10. 12

It's about the size of... 5

It's kind of like a... 5

It's like a... 13

It's similar to a... 13

It's so ... 5

It's used for...13

You use it for... 13

Really? I had a different experience. 18

Remember how I was (going to go to law school)? 17

Remember you have to (come home next week). 15

Sometimes, but not very often. 16

Let me check. It's about (10:45). 12

Let's do something special. 6

Let's go to dinner and a concert. F5-9

Let's see Mystery Date. 6

Make sure you see (the Statue of Liberty). 14

Maybe I can help. 13

Maybe some other time. 6

Maybe you should ask (name). 13

Maybe you should call someone since we can't make it work. F10-13

OK. I think I can find it. 11

Should we ask someone where it is? F 10-13

Sorry, could you say that again? 2

Sorry, I don't know what that's called. 13

Sorry, I'd rather not talk about it. 17

Sorry. You'll have to turn it off. 18

Thanks for asking, but I can't. 6

Thanks for inviting me over. 12

Thanks for noticing. 3

Thanks for your help. 11

Thanks, I got it. F1-4

Thanks, it's been fun talking with you. 15

Thanks, that helps me a lot. 11

Turn left on (Fifth) and you will see (the building on your right). 11

Walk for about (1 minute/100 meters). 11

We could go out for dinner. 6

We could put it on our credit card. 9

Well, (dear), how is (Florence)? 15

Well, I think she's pretty. 10

Well, it's not that interesting. 16

What about you? 17

What are you talking about? 9

What do you call it? 13

What does it look like? 5

What is (that cord) used for? F 10-13

What kind do you want? 6

What time is it? 12

What was it like? 17

What's it like? 8

What's that in your hand? 5

What's the (agency's) phone number? F1-4

What's the name of the machine that you use to...? 13

What's your phone number? 2

When's the best time to call you? 2

Where are you going? 14

Where are you? 11

Where is it in (your room)? 8

Where's that? 14

Where's the (hotel we are staying at)? F10-13

Which (CD) did you buy? F1-4

Who did you go with? 4

Who is that man (wearing sunglasses)? 10

Would you like to go to a movie or a play? F5-9

Wow, that sounds interesting. Do you enjoy it? 16

You have to (pour in some water) before (you turn it on). 13

You look worried. Can I help you with anything? 13

You've been a big help, thanks. 11

PERSONAL QUESTIONS FOR CONVERSATION

Are you going to (Maui) or (Oahu)? 14

Are people from (the warmer parts of your country) more (expressive)? 10

Are there any machines that you can't use although (you would like to)? F10-13

Are you a (workaholic)? 16

Are you going to ask her out again? 18

Are you in the (art department)? 1

Are you interested in (music)? F1-4

Are you married? 1

Are you still living here in town? F14-18

Are you still living in (Boston)? 17

Can you describe one room in your house? F5-9

Could you move to another country and live there forever? F5-9

Did you enjoy it? 16

Did you do anything this weekend? 4

Did you have a nice weekend? F1-4

Did you see a movie? F1-4

Didn't you just move in? 8

Do people in your city have a special accent? 15

Do you enjoy your job? F14-18

Do you ever work with the film directors? 16

Do you have a part-time or full-time job? F14-18

Do you have any memories of those days? 17

Do you know a good place to go to practice my English? F14-18

Do you know a good place to meet English speakers? F5-9

Do you know any "workaholics"? What are they like? 16

Do you know anything about (place)? 9

Do you know anything about this (model of car)? F5-9

Do you like computers or are you scared of them? F10-13

Do you like it? F1-4

Do you like to go shopping? F5-9

Do you like visiting big cities? F14-18

Do you like your new apartment? 8

Do you like your job? 1

Do you live alone or with people? F5-9

Do you lose things very often? F5-9

Do you make a good salary? 1

Do you mind telling me about the first time you (got in trouble)? 17

Do you miss (China)? 7

Do you prefer any special types of (clothes)? 3

Do you really think she's (attractive)? 10

Do you remember (Stan)? What ever happened to him? F14-18

Do you remember any (childhood rhymes or songs)? 17

Do you remember anything about it? 17

Do you remember your first (heartbreak)? F14-18

Do you spend a lot of time (studying)? 12

Do you still get homesick? 7

Do you think he was (happy)? 9

Do you think it will be crowded? F10-13

Do you think it's important to be fashionable? F14-18

Do you think kids should be able to (pierce their bodies)? F14-18

Do you think that (smoking in public) is OK? F14-18

Do you think we should (meet them again)? F 10-13

Do you think young children should have (a computer to do their homework on)? F 10-13

Do you want to (go to Bali)? F14-18

Does she have a (boyfriend)? 10

Don't you think that (it's dangerous)? 15

Have you ever met a famous person? F10-13

Have you ever seen anyone with such (beautiful, long hair)? 10

How is your family? 1

How are people in the different parts of your country different? 10

How are you going to afford that? 9

How do you like living (working) here? 1

How do you like this (school)? 1

How is your (job)? 1

How is your (school work) going? 1

How long did you work at (Sybase)? F14-18

How many times do you (eat out) in a month? F5-9

How much time do you spend (watching TV)? 12

How much time do you spend (with your kids)? F10-13

How often do you (talk to people in English)? F1-4

How was your weekend? 4

I think he's (nice). What do you think? 10

I've been meaning to ask you: What do you think of (living in Rio de Janeiro)? 15

If you could go back to being a child, would you? F14-18

If you don't mind my asking, what's difficult about it? 15

If you had to (go there) who would you choose (to go with)? 9

Is having a lot of money important to you? F5-9

Is it unusual in any way? 11

Is it what you expected? 15

Is that a full time or a part time job? 16

Is this your first conference? 16

Now that you are settled in, what do you think of...? 5

Really, you're going to (run in the New York marathon)? 18

Tell me about (your dad). What's he like? F5-9

That depends. How much do you want to spend? F10-13

Wasn't she an interesting person? 18

What advice would you give a ("workaholic" friend)? 16

What are some "must have" items among your friends? 15

What are some good questions to ask at a first meeting? 1

What are some ways to do it? 2

What are the best ways to meet people who speak English? 1

What are you going to do in Paris? 14

What are you going to do there? 14